Wall of Flames

The Minnesota Forest Fire of 1894

Lawrence H. Larsen

The North Dakota Institute for Regional Studies

Fargo

Library of Congress Catalog Card Number: 84-61133
ISBN 0-911042-29-6

To Martha Kimberly

Contents

Northeast Minnesota

railroad – – – –

Duluth

13

Superior

Cloquet

Carlton

25

Kettle River Village

36

15

Willow River

4 Kerrick

Rutledge

3 12

Finlayson 4 7 Partridge

Miller 2 Kettle River Bridge

Grindstone Lake 2

Skunk lake Sandstone

7 9

Hinckley

#45 jumps tracks 3

Pokegama 8 Mission Creek

12

Mora 11

Pine City

18

Milaca 9

28

Rush City

St. Cloud

30

55

40

Elk River

30

Minneapolis St. Paul

N

Eastern Minnesota RR

St. Paul & Duluth RR

Mississippi River

St. Croix River

Wisconsin

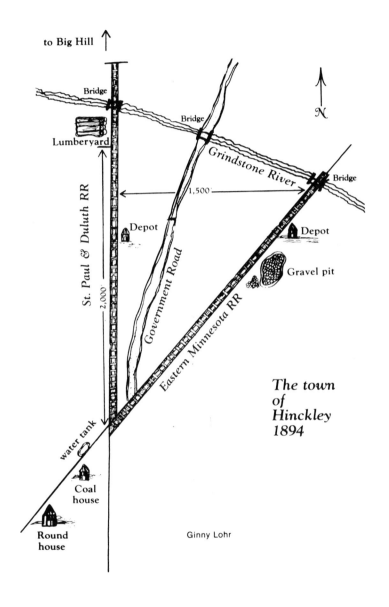

to Big Hill ↑

Bridge

Lumberyard

St. Paul & Duluth RR

← 1,500 →

Grindstone River

Bridge

N ↑

Bridge

Depot

2,000

Depot

Government Road

Gravel pit

Eastern Minnesota RR

The town of Hinckley 1894

water tank

Coal house

Round house

Ginny Lohr

Kettle River Village ●

15

Fire Zone

Willow River ●

4   Kerrick ●

Rutledge
3   12

Finlayson ●
4   7   Partridge ●
Miller ●   Kettle River Bridge
Grindstone Lake ○ 2   2
Skunk lake ●   Sandstone
7   9

Hinckley ●
#45 jumps tracks   3
Pokegama ●   8   Mission Creek

12   11

Mora ●
8   Pine City ●

9

Milaca ●

Rush City ●

36

Wisconsin

N

Eastern Minnesota RR

St. Paul & Duluth RR

Preface

On 1 September 1894 a murderous juggernaut of flames swept through the Minnesota pineries. The huge fire storm, thirty miles wide and five miles high, advanced across the land at a rate of thirty miles an hour. It threw fireballs and embers thousands of feet ahead, spawning its own whirlwinds and tornadoes of fire. The released fury had the force of several Hiroshima-size atomic bombs. Startled survivors first saw the Red Demon in the form of a great black cloud stretching toward the heavens. Within hours whole towns and settlements lay in ruins; over 900 square miles of prime timber had been reduced to ashes. Hundreds of people died and thousands more lost their homes before the fire stopped in marshes and cutover along the Wisconsin border. The Red Demon had wrought one of the great natural disasters in American history.

The Minnesota Forest Fire received national and international publicity even before the last embers died. Banner headlines in the 3 September 1894 edition of the New York *Times* proclaimed: "HUNDREDS PERISH IN FOREST FIRES: Western Towns Destroyed and Citizens Burned to Death in Their Crumbling Houses. TERRIBLE SCENES OF SUFFERING AT HINCKLEY. The Minnesota Town Completely Wiped Out by the Flames, and Many of Its Inhabitants Perish." The London *Times* carried stories about the conflagration for a week. It was the first large forest fire ever covered in detail by the mass media. The only North American fire that had killed more people, the Peshtigo Fire of 1871 in Wisconsin, received almost no notice. Because it happened on the same day as the Chicago Fire, the nation paid scant attention to this disaster in a remote portion of the northeastern Wisconsin woodlands. Early press dispatches cautioned readers that reported death tolls of over a thousand, correct as it turned out, were probably greatly exaggerated. There were few witnesses, for the flames came at night, the scattered survivors who cowered in lakes and streams seeing little except sparks and red glows. Piles of charred bodies in the blackened woodlands turned the stomachs of the first rescue workers. No way existed to reconstruct the minute-by-minute course of the fire. The opposite was true in the Minnesota blaze. Because it occurred during daylight, hundreds escaped death, making it possible to piece together the course of events.

The fire is important to study. On one level it sheds light on the reason such tragedies happened all too frequently in the United States of the Gilded Age. On another, it helps us to understand the origins of the Minnesota conservation movement. Even though forest fires continued to ravage the state — 559 people died in the Moose Lake disaster of 1918 — officials no longer treated them as normal phenomena. Yet the Minnesota Forest Fire's greatest significance was on the human level. It demonstrated how people, many ordinary and some important, responded to sudden adversity. Despite the horror of the moment, a triumph of the spirit happened in Minnesota in the long-ago summer of 1894. It is a story for all times, one that transcends events in the Minnesota north country.

Many people helped me with the project. Although it is impossible to mention all of them by name, I appreciate their contributions and advice. Some people were of particular help. Over the years, William Petrowski offered succinct observations concerning the project's historical worth and possibilities. William E. Lass helped in the early stages, providing valuable advice on the location of materials. Fredrick Spletstoser, Stanley B. Parsons, R. Reed Whitaker, Patrick McLear, and Richard Elrod made pertinent suggestions. So did Roger T. Johnson, Gerald Kennan, Stephen Cox, George Gale, and Daniel Jaffe. Marilyn Lass of the Minnesota Room at Mankato State University was of immense aid. I also acknowledge the efforts of professional staff members at the Minnesota State Historical Society and at the library of Bemidji State University. At the latter institution, Mrs. Charles Holt was especially helpful in regard to newspaper holdings. My wife, Barbara J. Cottrell, was a major contributor. James and Marian Cottrell provided an island in Canada. Dean Eldon Parizek of the University of Missouri-Kansas City nurtured an increasingly scholarly environment. Elizabeth McIntyre and Barbara LoCascio typed the manuscript.

Of course (though both custom and prudence demand it be said), I am responsible for errors of fact or interpretation.

Lawrence H. Larsen

Chapter 1
"The Red Demon of the North"

On 16 July 1894 the Minneapolis *Tribune* carried a short dispatch concerning the woodlands some seventy miles north of Minneapolis-St. Paul. Datelined Hinckley, it read: "The forest fires in this vicinity continue, and along the lines of the Eastern Minnesota the property of the country is threatened to such an extent that the section men are all out fighting the flames. So far no reports have been received of any damage to buildings, although in several instances the fires have approached very closely, and have only been driven back after hard fighting. Along the line of the St. Paul and Duluth, between this place and Mission Creek, the next station south of here, there has been considerable loss from the fires in the meadows, hundreds of tons of hay having been destroyed. It has not yet been necessary for the company to take any steps to protect its property, as the fires have been some distance from its right-of-way. Unless a heavy rain comes soon there will be great loss sustained, as the fires are spreading rapidly, and everything is as dry as tinder."

While the report caused apprehension, few persons believed the situation alarming. Fires always occurred in the vast pine forests of Minnesota. Every summer a characteristic haze hung over many parts of the state, diffusing the sun's rays. On a supposedly clear day the sky frequently appeared low and ominous. An almost continual trace of wood smoke hung in the air, a condition the inhabitants took for granted. It had been an accepted part of life since the 1860s when promoters had first thrust railroads into the lumber regions. After the establishment of lumber camps and the construction of sawmills, the tracks became the arteries of commerce that carried Minnesota lumber throughout the rest of the country, and the world for that matter. As early as 1873, millions of feet of wood flowed southward from what were little more than place names with a mill: 1.4 million feet from North Branch, 3.7 million from

Pine City, and 5.9 million from Hinckley. Twenty years later, and even before the exploitation of the far northern counties of Beltrami and Koochiching, the production figures for Minnesota, as well as those for Wisconsin and Michigan, reflected a massive effort to fulfill the needs of America's industrial and urban revolutions. Shipments from Minneapolis in 1892 amounted to almost 400 million feet. Totals for individual lumber companies frequently exceeded 20 million feet. At Hinckley, the mill owned by the Brennan Lumber Company annually produced 31.7 million feet of lumber products. The Laird, Norton Company owned thousands of acres of trees in the vicinity.[1] Lumbering had become a big and profitable business, creating numerous towns and employing thousands of lumberjacks and woodworkers. It made fortunes for the Weyerhaeusers, the Lairds, and the Atwoods. In their eyes it led to human progress; in those of reformers it created a generation of vicious, predatory, and irresponsible lumber barons who raped the natural resources of the Upper Midwest for their own personal gain.

The lumber companies' methods created conditions in the pineries that had never before existed. Lumberjacks systematically felled trees selected and marked by inspectors called timber cruisers, a crude form of tree harvesting. Unless the land had obvious agricultural value, which it usually did not, being sandy and covered with stones, the cruisers selected only mature trees for cutting. A fir left unharvested until it reached old age became infested with large white worms and a multitude of smaller insects. Considered delicacies by hairy woodpeckers, the worms destroyed the timber's commercial value. The lumber companies did not spare young trees for conservation reasons, considering it not worth the effort. The woodmen's axes had as targets the stately white pines, Norway pines, spruces, birches, and Douglas firs, almost all two or more feet in diameter. Crews chopped down virgin timber during the summer months and left it to dry. In the winter, farmers supplemented their incomes by hauling logs to the mills. Usually, they used teams of horses, which they could maneuver under snowy conditions on the uneven surface and in the close spaces of the forest. Contrary to folk tales about Paul Bunyan and his Blue Ox, they seldom employed oxen extensively. Clumsy and of low intelligence, the formidable-appearing beasts had negligible worth in close quarters. Before moving the logs, workers cut away the slashings. These remained behind on the forest floor, mingling with windfalls and dead timber and severely altering environmental conditions. This practice greatly increased the fire danger.

There are three types of forest fires.[2] Ground fires smoulder beneath the surface, feeding on peat, humus, and root systems. Such blazes eat their way along for a considerable period of time, eventually stopping. Most start unnoticed and die the same way. Sometimes, they break through to the forest floor, causing a surface fire. This kind, which can start in a variety of ways, destroys the underbrush. These fires are normally beneficial and in harmony with nature's balance. Certain seeds germinate after a fire has passed through. Flames can ignite the needles high in the trees, resulting in a crown fire. This spectacular and menacing conflagration can develop a life of its own, creating turbulence and jumping along virtually independent of ground and surface fires. While a crown fire almost always will burn out or is contained by quick countermeasures, there are exceptions. When this happens, a major disaster can follow.

Climatic disturbances increase the danger: a change in wind velocity might turn a minor blaze into a raging menace; extended droughts make forests susceptible to the torch. The worst, a temperature inversion, exists when a layer of cool air forms above one of warm air. The temperature on the ground is hot, the atmosphere muggy, and the wind still, causing smoke and other pollution to hang in the air. Indians recorded the phenomenon in the 1600s in the Los Angeles basin, where it frequently happens. Ordinarily, the inversion breaks with blessed relief for those affected. But a fire can create a "blow-up." All fires have convection columns. They make their own wind and have the capacity to break through the inversion, much like a boxer punching a hole in a ceiling. A dormant fire can ignite in great fury and explode up through the open flue. This is bad enough, but when coupled with a combination of a sudden high ground wind and a large number of fires fighting for air, the consequences are catastrophic. A fire storm sweeps forward throwing fireballs, embers, and objects thousands of feet ahead. No one has discovered a way to stop this Red Demon. It consumes everything in its path, trapping those who stay to fight or who are slow in escaping. Huge bubbles of gas travel upward in the tornado-like column, which may reach up five miles. The whirlwinds at the core move in a clockwise direc-

4

tion, leaping ahead, leaving some places untouched and turning others into cinders. The unleashed fury reaches the force of several Hiroshima-type atomic bombs. For obvious reasons, not enough is known about the horrible juggernauts: no sensible observer capable of getting away lingers to record eyewitness recollections for posterity.

Fire storms caused major havoc in North America during the nineteenth century. No one had the means to predict when and where one would occur. After all, fires broke out daily for years in Chicago prior to Mrs. O'Leary's obstinate cow supposedly kicking over a lantern. And the kind of climatic conditions that prevailed on the Chicago evening of 8 October 1871 — hot and oppressively muggy with a brisk southwestern wind — were not unusual during Indian Summer in the Midwest. The same weather had occurred the previous night, when firemen contained a blaze that destroyed many blocks. The O'Leary fire differed because for unknown reasons its convection tower fought up through the inversion and became a wave of flames that moved across the Windy City, burning the downtown district and the docks and destroying over 40,000 dwellings. Although early wire dispatches incorrectly said the whole city had gone up in flames, over 160,000 of 350,000 residents lost their homes and total losses amounted to $196 million.[3]

Forty-six years earlier, almost to the day, on 7 October 1825, a similar fire ravaged New Brunswick in the Maritimes, burning 10,000 out of 25,000 miles of territory. Completely laying waste the commercial city of Newcastle, the fire cut a wide swath through the capital, Fredericton. Several hundred souls perished in remote farms and lumber camps throughout the British colony. For days prior to the disaster, fires in the forests and air charged with wood smoke had caused little apprehension, considered a necessary part of land-clearance projects. With startling suddenness, the flames merged in mid-morning into a "most impetuous hurricane" that quickly did its terrible work. Sir Howard Douglas-Bart, the lieutenant governor, wrote his superiors in London, "I wish I could report that life has been spared, but so violently driven were the flames and embers from the blazing woods, well prepared for the most combustion by the largest season of heat and drought ever known, that men, women and children in great numbers have perished in the towns and in the woods, in exertions to save property, or in attempts to save life; and when driven in terror to seek safety on the water, greater numbers still appear to have suffered in attempts to cross the rivers in boats or in canoes, or rafts or on logs of timber, which were alike incapable of resisting the fury of the storm." He said that a gale blew out of the northwest, just before the conflagration reached Fredericton, and, without understanding the scientific reasons, recorded the classic elements of a fire storm: "As evening advanced the woods, which had continued to burn throughout the day, were now distinctly seen to be everywhere burning, and vast clouds of smoke, rising in the distance, accompanied by extraordinary noises, as of furious explosions of flame, and the fire reflected on the distant sky, portended other calamities."[4] For days afterwards ash particles dropped from the sky over Boston, New York, and other Eastern Seaboard localities in the United States. During the same decade a smoky haze from large fires in the West passed over the Northeast, but no one has any way of knowing if fire storms bore the responsibility.

A massive temperature inversion covered the Midwest in early October of 1871, making Chicago only one of several places that experienced a disaster. The Peshtigo fire in northeastern Wisconsin burned 1,182 people to death, as high winds drove the flames over several thousand square miles in less than two hours.[5] If a similar gale had struck at Chicago, 100,000 instead of 250 persons might have perished. Other blazes burned out of control in Windsor, Ontario. A conflagration in Michigan, that started in the Lower Peninsula around Holland, Grand Haven, and Manistee, swept across the state in an easterly direction. Forest fires of great strength devoured timber lands in unsettled portions of Minnesota and western Ontario. A massive pall of smoke lay like a shroud across the region. Terror gripped the hearts of countless thousands before the skies cleared, the embers died, and the rebuilding began. Reconstruction proceeded so quickly in Chicago that in a few years hardly any traces of the fire remained. Ignoring the lessons of what had happened there and elsewhere, the people went back about their business and treated the whole affair as an isolated phenomenon, or, in the case of Peshtigo, as wanton carelessness punished by an avenging God. No one analyzed why so many fires happened at different areas at the same time, passing it off as a remarkable coincidence. In Chicago a cow rather than nature received the blame, the myth remaining prevalent over a hundred years afterwards.

On 5 September 1881 a forest fire in eastern Michigan burned through four heavily timbered counties, killing 125 people and threatening Port Huron. Because of persistent unverified reports that attributed the fire to climatic conditions, the United States Army Signal Service undertook an investigation. Sergeant William Bailey, appointed to head the inquiry, found the familiar elements: unseasonably dry weather and numerous small fires due to a hot summer and below-normal rainfall. Although newspaper accounts of small blazes in the slashings and underbrush evoked concern, no one considered the situation serious enough to take corrective action. In August the earth cracked; the swamps dried and baked into hard clay. On the fateful day, hurricane-force winds roared from the southwest, uprooting eight-inch trees. The temperature in the shade hovered around 100 °F. The conclusion seemed obvious — it should be a crime to start blazes recklessly in warm seasons and authorities must take concerted steps to stop forest fires.[6]

Christopher C. Andrews was a distinguished Minnesotan. At the start of the Civil War, at thirty-two years of age, he abandoned a career as a newspaper commentator and lawyer in St. Cloud to enter service as a captain of volunteers in the Third Minnesota Infantry. Soon reaching colonel, by the end of hostilities he had achieved the rank of brigadier general. In 1868 he ran for Congress on the Republican ticket and lost; the next year President Ulysses S. Grant appointed him minister to Sweden and Norway. Andrews represented the United States in Stockholm for eight and a half years, gaining a reputation as a capable and conscientious envoy. He learned Swedish, wrote more than thirty reports published by the United States government, studied the Swedish iron ore industry, and became enamored of Scandinavian forestry practices. The numerous checkerboard forests, with trees in different stages of growth, impressed him the most.

By the time Andrews returned to Minnesota and settled in

St. Paul, he had become an ardent conservationist: his experiences abroad had convinced him of the need for scientific forest management. While he believed in preventing fires, he thought in broader environmental terms than simply leaving all growth in a virgin state. "Many people think that forest conservation means leaving all trees standing," he said in his memoirs. "This is a mistake. Timber should be cut when it is ripe, or has ceased to earn good interest by its growth. Much of the present pine forest in the Northwest has been growing for one to three hundred years. It should be cut as fast as there is a market for it. When pine is cut, all seedlings should be protected so that they may reach their full growth."[7] In 1880 he persuaded the St. Paul Chamber of Commerce to petition Congress in what proved an unsuccessful effort to establish a national school of forestry. Two years later he read a scholarly paper calling for timber reform before a forestry convention in Cincinnati. A lifelong Republican, Andrews disagreed with the party's opposition to massive federal intervention into forestry matters; rather, he admired the conservation reforms that Democrat Grover Cleveland accomplished as governor of New York and later as President of the United States.

Many people believed Andrews would give up his "hobby" after he accepted an appointment as consul general in Rio de Janeiro. He held that post from 1882 to 1887, writing a book, *Brazil: Its Conditions and Prospects* (New York, 1887). After returning to Minnesota, Andrews continued to campaign for forest reform. Believing that the lumber companies would soon deplete the state's timber resources if they continued to have their way, he also clearly perceived the danger from leaving untold millions of feet of dry slashings in the woodlands. The state had little forestry legislation. The Minnesota State Forestry Association, interested in planting trees, had persuaded the 1873 legislature to pass a "Tree Bounty Law" that offered farmers $2.50 an acre to plant groves. The measure had hardly any impact, with only 65,000 acres reforested during the following thirty-five years. Another measure, making it a crime to start a forest fire, went unenforced. In 1892 the Populist party registered major gains in the state legislature in Minnesota with a platform calling for planned forest management, for water-management controls, for checking timber monopolies, and for fire prevention. But nothing came of it — the lumber interests had too much strength and influence.

In an effort to advocate his beliefs, Andrews submitted several papers to the American Forestry Association. One, read on 22 August 1894 before a meeting of the association in Brooklyn, New York, bore the title, "The Prevention of Forest Fires." He emphasized the need for a system of fire wardens and lookout towers, but, as almost all scholarly papers, it went unnoticed. Three weeks later, his comments appeared in an article published in the *Northwestern Agriculturalist*. By then things had changed.[8]

In 1894 drought conditions compounded the exigencies of a long and hot summer in the Upper Midwest. Cursing the weather, farmers looked skyward and despaired for their crops. In August the *Monthly Weather Review*, issued by the United States Department of Agriculture, claimed that poor conditions plagued the region for several reasons. The adverse circumstances, however, had not come overnight; they related to a long period of insufficient rainfall. "The tables of accumulated precipitation published monthly, show that the whole region in which the crops have suffered during August, reports a steady and generally increasing deficiency in the accumulated rainfall since the first of January," the editor commented. "The drouth is, therefore, not merely the drouth of July and August, but that of several months."[9] The dry bureaucratic prose forecast trouble in the Minnesota pineries. The leaves on bushes, plants, and seedlings withered and died, pine needles crackled underfoot, and the air lost its usual stimulating summer briskness. Anglers blamed their failures on the weather, as water levels dropped in streams, lakes, and marshes. Hundreds of small fires smouldered and flared.

Records kept by the St. Paul weather bureau made for grim reading. The normal rainfall from 16 May to 10 September was 13.61". Only 2.20" fell during the same period in 1894, a deficiency of 11.41" and 84 percent below normal. At the same time, the temperature reached 4.2 °F above normal. In July St. Paul recorded its highest mean ever. The humidity for the summer of 1894 averaged 60.5 percent in June, 48 percent in July, and 59.6 percent in August. During 1891, a summer with a normal rainfall, the humidity averaged 77 percent in June, 81 percent in July, and 74 percent in August. The winds were light from

9 June through 31 August, 1894, coming, as usual, generally out of the southeast or northwest. This constituted the only normal aspect of the summer — no high and hot winds helped dry the forest. It made little difference. The poor rainfall, the abnormally high temperatures, and the low humidity combined to make the woods ready for burning.[10]

Pine County covered 1,400 square miles of eastern Minnesota, hard against the Wisconsin border. With a shape much like that of the state of Maine, the county had a narrow lower portion that expanded rectangularly in the upper two-thirds. Pine County's center lay seventy miles south of Duluth-Superior and eighty miles north of Minneapolis-St. Paul. Most of the undulating and rolling rocky land consisted of pine barrens, swamps, and twenty-six lakes. A large number of streams emptied into the Kettle and St. Croix rivers. While much timber remained, a great deal had been cut in the seventies and eighties. By 1894 the lumber concerns had started to calculate when operations would become unprofitable and they would find it expedient to move on. Axes had felled most of the virgin wood — gigantic pines that rose 100 to 150 feet, with interlocking branches that created a vast canopy.[11]

Census statistics detailed the county's development. With only 62 residents in 1860 and 648 in 1870, the county grew rapidly with the coming of the railroads and the timber-cutting operations, reaching 1,365 in 1880 and 4,052 in 1890. Native-born totaled 2,222 and foreign-born 1,830. The immigrants included 966 Swedes, 272 Canadians, 253 Norwegians, and 215 Germans, with smaller numbers of Poles (92), Irish (78), English (52), Dutch (37), and Danes (27). Enumerated among the native-born were 135 Indians and 141 "colored." Throughout the county there were 2,350 males and 1,702 females. Native-born males aggregated 1,216 and females, 1,006. Foreign-born computations showed 1,134 males and 696 females. Overall, the figures gave truth to the observation that a society based on lumbering was a man's world. Seven hundred and fifty-seven dwellings housed 781 families, persons per dwelling averaging 5.35. There were many youths and young adults: some 1,246 individuals were between the ages of five and twenty. Of the 1,290 males twenty-one and over, 377 were born in the United

States and 913 outside the country. Obviously, the immigrant stock comprised the backbone of the work force. As might have been expected, organized religion was far from a pervasive element, there being twenty organizations, ten churches, and 877 communicants. The population count for Pine County mirrored that of Minnesota as a whole, which grew from 781,000 in 1880 to 1.3 million in 1890, when 62.6 million people lived in the United States.[12]

In 1890 Pine County did not rank as an important agricultural area, having only 201 farms. By way of contrast, Minnesota's southern Dakota County contained 1,880 farms and northern Beltrami County had 56. Other statistical indicators further demonstrated how little Pine County contributed to the state's agricultural base. It had 202 of 461,409 horses, 303 of 9,315 mules, 416 of 853,715 swine, 4,602 of 4,448,831 chickens, 99 of 151,000 turkeys, 120 of 69,224 geese, and 57 of 74,697 ducks. Cereal crops were paltry — 328 bushels of barley, 489 of buckwheat, 6,240 of Indian corn, 9,995 of oats, 532 of rye, and 1,590 of wheat. Hay production came to 2,412 tons and Irish potatoes to 38,897 pounds. Fewer than 4,000 acres were under cultivation,[13] the rocky and light soil in the pine barrens defying the plow.

The industrial schedules in the 1890 census failed to convey the significant role played by the county in the American economy. The rolls enumerated ten establishments that had a capital of $986,000. There were live assets of $548,000 and miscellaneous expenses of $40,000. The cost of materials was $326,000; the value of products $635,000. An average of 340 employees earned $108,000 in annual wages, none of the workers being under sixteen years old.[14] So stated the cold statistical compilations. They failed to reveal, however, that almost all the industrial firms were lumber mills that cut millions of feet of wood every year. Surely, the figures seemed low and suspect.

In 1890 Pine County had no urban sites, using the then-standard census definition of 2,500 people as the breaking point between rural and urban political units. The largest villages were Hinckley with 618 people, Pine City with 535, and Sandstone with 517. During formulative periods, population figures poorly indicated social and material progress, even though they were consistently used as such in the nineteenth century. The key to eventual urban ascendancy was the ability to attract and generate enough capital to sustain economic growth. Here, one place in Pine County appeared to enjoy an advantage. Hinckley, the county seat, had become the center of lumbering operations and the key railroad junction. Though most of the profits from lumbering went elsewhere, there was enough business to generate progress. The community grew markedly after 1890, having an estimated 1894 population of 1,200. In the same span, Sandstone fell back and Pine City rose slightly. Even though the lumber industry in the area appeared on the wane, the sheer concentration of people helped Hinckley. It had no chance of becoming a major city because of the proximity of Duluth-Superior and Minneapolis-St. Paul. These larger units dominated Minnesota's economy. However, Hinckley had the opportunity to achieve the status of a St. Cloud, Mankato, or Rochester, to become an important local marketing center. That was the way it was on 31 August 1894.

Railroads were tremendously important to Pine County, single-track trunks setting the economic and social rhythm. Without them there would have been no practicable way to ship lumber to market, and possibly no Pine County. While the railroads brought in almost all products and produce, they also served as the most convenient and quickest way to reach distant points. Shrill whistles, clanging bells, chugging engines, and rattling cars frequently broke the forest stillness, as clouds of black smoke trailed the great black engines. Fast passengers and slow freights operated on regular schedules. The arrival of the daily mail, which usually came in the afternoon, marked an important event in a small town, many people finding excuses to be at the station to watch and listen. They broke the monotony of everyday life by paying close attention to whether or not the train arrived on time, how many cars the engine pulled, who got on and off, and the quantity of freight unloaded. And, they might be among the first to obtain a metropolitan newspaper — the Minneapolis *Tribune*, the St. Paul *Pioneer Press*, or the Duluth *News Tribune*. The train might even take on fuel and water. After a time, the conductor, the regal official in dark blue who controlled the train's movements, would study his watch, signal "All aboard," and climb on after it had already started to move. After the engine and cars had rumbled down the line, the spectators went back to their routine activities, planning to repeat the process the following day. While persons pretended to take the greatest transportation innovation of the nineteenth century for granted, deep down they thought trains something special.

The St. Paul & Duluth Railroad ran almost directly north and south through Pine County. Built by Minneapolis-St. Paul business interests, it carried millions of barrels of Minneapolis flour to the lake head in Duluth-Superior for shipment east through the Great Lakes. Of course, it also hauled huge amounts of lumber. Covering the shortest route between St. Paul and Duluth, the "Skalley," as local people called the line, operated high-speed passenger service between the two points. A couple of trains daily moved in both directions. Leaving Duluth every day promptly at 1:55 p.m. the crack southbound limited, designated Passenger Train No. 4, shot south, rolling into Pine County and arriving at Hinckley at 4:05 p.m. In keeping with the practices for fast trains, the railroad did everything humanly and technically possible to stay on time. Smoke from the many fires burning in the summer of 1894 failed to interfere with the regular schedules. Because the crew considered fires routine and saw no need to slow down, No. 4 ran through the affected areas at normal speeds. It took more than a few black clouds to stop an express on the St. Paul & Duluth line.

The Eastern Minnesota Railway, a division of James J. Hill's Great Northern system, cut through Pine County from the northeast at a little less than a 45° angle. Hill ranked as one of the leading business organizers in the country. A massive and muscular man of over 300 pounds, he built a transcontinental without aid from the federal government at a time when most railroad men felt such help necessary for large projects. A ruthless Robber Baron to some, he was the Empire Builder to others, the person most responsible for settling the Northwest. He knew the Eastern Minnesota like the back of his hand: it was one of his prime railway properties. The road ran out of Duluth-Superior, moved down through first Carlton County and then Pine County. It turned west into Kanabec and Mille Lacs counties, splitting at Milaca, an obscure connection point. One line thrust twenty-eight miles on to St. Cloud, where it joined the Great Northern's main line. The other swung sixty miles south to St. Paul. No. 4 down limited passenger train, which bore the same number as the afternoon St. Paul & Duluth train, left Duluth for St. Paul at 1:00 p.m. It roared south, arriving at 3:25 p.m. at Hinckley where it passed the daily West Superior-Hinckley freight. This train, No. 23 on the down run, then became No. 24 and immediately returned north. No. 4, after refueling and switching, continued on toward St. Paul.[15] It was all routine. The men on the Eastern Minnesota considered themselves in competition with those on the St. Paul & Duluth, and they took pride in running on time. A few blazes in the pineries amounted to nothing more than minor inconveniences.

The two railroads crossed in Hinckley's southern outskirts, the St. Paul & Duluth going straight south, the Eastern Minnesota cutting across in a gradual turn from the northeast. Hinckley had acquired the yards and roundhouse associated with a junction point. Hardly ranking with Chicago or Kansas City, the facilities made Hinckley the rail center of Pine County. Furthermore, numerous railroad workers lived in the village.

As the lines moved south from Duluth-Superior they slashed through the heart of the lumber regions. Thirty-six miles from the two ports the Eastern Minnesota reached Kerrick, a station in northern Pine County. The next sixteen miles contained nineteen bridges and heavy timber on both sides of the right-of-way. Twelve miles down the track on this stretch was a lumber camp, Partridge. Fifty people lived in the vicinity of the grubby little station house. Seven miles farther on flowed the 300-foot wide Kettle River, bridged by a gigantic wooden trestle 850 feet long and 132 feet high at its highest point. Watchmen with headquarters at the south end of the structure regulated all traffic, rigidly enforcing a company-imposed four miles-per-hour speed limit. Two miles down the line came Sandstone, where most of the adults in the prosperous village of more than 500 worked in the nearby quarries. Sandstone had several impressive buildings, including a large schoolhouse. From there, it was nine miles to Hinckley, then on to Pokegama station, eight miles slightly southwest of Hinckley on the western edge of Pine County. The promoters had high hopes for the little lumber camp, which had the post office address of Brook Park. Another lumber siding, Mora, was twelve miles away, and eighteen miles after that the tracks reached the Milaca junction.

The St. Paul & Duluth swung slightly west out of Duluth to the prosperous Carlton County lumber town of Cloquet, about eighteen miles down the line. In the next twenty-five miles the tracks passed through Carlton, Thompson, and Barnum, reaching the village of Kettle River. The rails then dropped thirty-five miles almost straight south into Pine County, passing three stations, Rutledge, Finlayson Depot, and Miller, before arriving in Hinckley. Three miles farther south lay Mission Creek, a small lumber camp. Most trains did not stop, continuing another eleven miles to much larger Pine City, then another nine miles from there to Rush City, and fifty-five more to the depot in St. Paul.[16]

Hinckley's reason for existence was the Brennan Lumber Company. The town, originally called Central Station, and renamed after a Pennsylvania Railroad director, held no importance until 1874 when Thomas Brennan decided the site, on the south bank of the Grindstone River, ideal for a sawmill. Hinckley was situated near the confluence of the stream's north and south branches, both of which came out of Lake Grindstone in Pine County's higher elevations. Logs from the pineries could be stored in the lake, floated down the river, dried in the yards, cut to specifications, and shipped out by rail. Brennan built a mill that developed into one of Minnesota's largest. At first, George Turner of Minneapolis provided most of the logs. When his firm depleted its holdings, the Lairds and Nortons of Winona and the Staples of Stillwater furnished almost all the timber fed into the huge circular saws. After he established a large retail yard in St. Paul, Brennan sold his Hinckley holdings in 1889 to a syndicate of Eau Claire, Wisconsin, lumbermen. The sawmill burned within a few weeks, but the new owners quickly rebuilt. Between 300 and 400 men worked for the Brennan Lumber Company, cutting 200,000 feet of wood daily.[17] While the workers might curse their lot and denounce the Lumber Kings, few of them worried about the forests being denuded and the mill forced to close. Mostly transients, they took eventually moving on for granted — to Idaho, Oregon, Washington, or British Columbia. It was the way of the industry.

Lumber towns were crude, and Hinckley was no exception. It lay in cutover cleared by the Brennan Lumber Company, no one having given much thought to planning or, for that matter, to permanence. Hinckley was a far cry from the thoughtful and deliberate attempts of the first American industrialists in Massachussetts to create "cities in nature" with pleasant surroundings that would serve as monuments to the glories of capitalism and the correct way to conduct an industrial revolution devoid of the suffering so common in the factory warrens of the United Kingdom. Hinckley on the Grindstone had nothing in common with Lowell on the Merrimack or Holyoke on the Connecticut. In Hinckley the owner had quickly cleared the site and proceeded accordingly — a few hastily graded streets, many jammed-together lots, a quick sale of land, and that was all. The results were as expected: awful and depressing. What could have been an idyllic and picturesque village in the wilderness became instead an uninviting group of buildings dissected by a few bumpy thoroughfares.

Almost completely flat, Hinckley, defying the surrounding rolling country, resembled a pool table. It had no trees for the lumbermen had cut the indigenous virgin pines and shipped them away. The tallest things in Hinckley were the telegraph poles, former tree trunks. No one cared about the lack of beautification. More or less by accident, the railroads had determined the town's basic shape. In a rather rough-and-ready fashion, the tracks acted as sort of unofficial city limits. The St. Paul & Duluth Railroad marked the western boundary, with only a few structures beyond the tracks. To the north the Grindstone River formed a natural limit. The Brennan Lumber Company, however, had retained a wide strip for expansion purposes, so the town started approximately 1,000 feet south of the river. The Eastern Minnesota entered Hinckley from the north, about 1,500 feet to the east of the St. Paul & Duluth, and cut diagonally toward the southwest. No buildings stood east of the Eastern Minnesota, only what even the residents of Hinckley considered an eyesore — an ugly three-acre gravel pit owned by the railroad. Despite frequent complaints, the line did nothing about the open excavation, the dirt and stone from which had gone to raise a long stretch of track. The Eastern Minnesota crossed the St. Paul & Duluth about 3,000 feet below the Grindstone River. The coal house and roundhouse stood just beyond the junction point in the yards, away from the built-up portions of Hinckley.

The developed town formed a triangle, roughly 1,500 feet at the top and about 2,000 feet between there and the base. In sharp deviation from normal town-building methods in the United States, Hinckley had no main business streets or town squares. Structures of all kinds intermingled: houses and saloons, eight stores and three churches, the Odd Fellows' Hall and houses of prostitution, warehouses and a school, all inside the compact environment dictated by the tracks. Fire posed a constant threat, even when the woods were wet, since the townspeople had constructed every building of wood. None stood more than two stories high, and almost all were rectangular in design. The biggest, the fifty-room Morrison Hotel, had six "kept" girls. It was a landmark, along with the two railroad stations, both located on the north side directly across town from each other. Another well-known building, the unoriginally named Eating House, contained the only decent place to get a good meal. Hinckley had neither electricity nor telephone service,[18] and wooden planks served as sidewalks. There were no sewers. Privies satisfied human needs; surface water and household wastes ran into the ground or swirled around on the surface. No systematic program of street-cleaning existed. Horses' hoofs supposedly worked manure into the surface. Drinking water came from either wells or the Grindstone River. With a population density about the same as that in Calcutta or Bombay, Hinckley was just another lumber town, a whole state of affairs familiar to lumberjacks.

On a hot Minnesota morning in the latter part of July 1894, Mrs. Lucy Kelsey received discouraging news while at the Great Northern ticket office on Nicollet Avenue in downtown Minneapolis: the 1:30 p.m. Duluth Limited on the Eastern Minnesota did not stop at Pokegama, her destination and future home. On her way to join her husband and oldest son, she had only her two smallest sons to worry about. She had left her oldest daughter at the family's old residence and the youngest girl had decided to remain temporarily in the Twin Cities. The ticket agent gave Lucy two alternatives: she and her sons could take the limited to Milaca, spend the night, and go on to Pokegama the next day on the local, or they could buy through tickets to Hinckley and try to get a wagon back from there, a distance of eight miles. Without much hesitation, she decided to purchase tickets to Hinckley. "As neither prospect seemed alluring," she declared, "I resolved to trust to the good nature of the conductor, and rested quietly in the conviction that I should not go on to Hinckley that day."

Her train clicked and clacked on schedule out of the Minneapolis Union Depot. It slowly bridged the Mississippi River,
rolled up the north bank for thirty miles, swung north at Elk
River, and started the thirty-mile run to Milaca, the beginning
of the lumber region — the "new country" that Lucy longed
to see. About fifteen miles south of Milaca the train chugged
into smoke. "Nowhere at that time did we see flames, but at
intervals it was evident that the woods were burning slowly,"
Lucy remembered. On one occasion the train halted, while the
crew removed a fallen tree from the track. After the train passed
Milaca, the conductor told Lucy that he would make a short
flag stop at Pokegama. She gathered her children and belongings, and waited on the car platform. The limited slowed to
a crawl and then halted in what appeared the middle of
nowhere. Before Lucy really realized what was happening, she
was standing beside the track watching the train disappear up
the line. She experienced the lonely feeling of suddenly being
left behind in the wilderness. "To my surprise, I seemed to have
been left to one side of the main settlement, how far, I knew
not," she recalled. "Before me stretched the interminable track."
The sun at 4:20 p.m. was still high in the sky; the air was hot
and charged with smoke. It was still and quiet, except for the
distant chugging of the limited. "I thought we were coming up
north," Lucy's small son, Earl, complained. She looked down
at him and said in a stern voice, "We are up north surely, and
perhaps we will find some one, if we keep up courage."

Lucy quickly realized that the train had dropped them off
to the west of Pokegama. The nearest building, a six-foot-square
line house, the railroad used for storing tools. A wagon road
wound off into the trees. Across a siding two seedy saloons
showed no signs of being open for business. She did not see a
single person — unusual, given that the train had stopped. Picking up the luggage, Lucy told her children to follow her up the
track. The three walked what seemed a mile, crossing a long
dam before reaching a high trestle around which lay a tiny settlement. It contained a steam sawmill, some log cabins, a combination store and post office, and a large frame house. Lucy,
identifying the latter building as a boarding house, walked up
to it and asked a woman standing on the porch, "Will you take
in some wayfarers?" The reply — coming in what previously
had appeared a hostile environment — was friendly and reassur-

ing: "Oh, yes. Your husband will be here soon." After that
matters went smoothly.

Lucy's new home, which her husband had constructed out
of solid blocks hewed from ash, tamarack, and basswood logs,
was down an "evergreen path." It had large windows on three
sides and two doors, one with an ornate gable above it. To the
south was a twelve-foot-deep well with a tight pine cover. In
that direction the trees had been cut for a distance of several
rods, most of the wood for the house having come from this
patch. On the north and the west large pines stood only a few
feet away. Immediately to the east many blackened and dead
trees served as a stark and grim reminder of an early July brush
fire that had burned out of control. Such an unsightly distrac-
tion did not bother Lucy, for she saw only beauty in her unique
forest fairyland. "Though at first glance it seemed as if we were
surrounded on all sides by an impenetrable forest, I soon found
a romantic logging road, winding through balsams, pines and
tamaracks as well as other native trees," she wrote. "The trees
arched so prettily that we called it the 'arched road.' This road
opened out into a beautiful meadow, through which flowed a
creek, now nearly dry in places. There was a shorter road to
the meadow through the blackened trees east, but this became
the favorite path."[19]

The Kelsey cabin was a fifteen- to twenty-five-minute walk
east of the center of Pokegama. Lucy, with her family gathered
around her, caught the spirit of creating a community in a forest
fastness. Her husband, C. W. Kelsey, hoped to participate in
the building of a great city, called Brook Park. He had a brother,
a physician turned land speculator, Dr. C. A. Kelsey, the principal promoter of Pokegama, who represented the Kelsey-
Markham Land Company. Dr. Kelsey and his three partners,
who included two of his brothers, owned 15,000 acres in the
vicinity.[20] Perhaps Lucy's attachment to the hamlet came too
quickly, a common phenomenon in the United States of the nineteenth century. It took an almost religious fervor and dedication to build a city. Even though Pokegama's prospects appeared
slim, who could really tell for sure? While it seemingly had no
hope of overcoming the obvious advantage held by nearby
Hinckley, there was always a slight chance. Such hope sustained
town promoters. Other Pokegama pioneers shared the same
dream: Alexander Berg, the store owner and postmaster; Hans
Nelson, the station agent for the Eastern Minnesota; and Mrs.

Carver, the boarding house keeper. Many families hoped to start lives anew. The Nelsons, the Andersons, the Frances, the Carvers, and the Batys were all Pokegama pioneers. A German Jewish family, the Bramans, worked industriously to improve their land. Their son, "Jakey," impressed everyone as a young man with a bright future. In August the men pitched together to construct a two-story schoolhouse, a symbol of community providing those involved in the construction with a feeling of pride and a sense of belonging. After they finished their work near the end of the month, they scheduled a short dedication ceremony for 1 September 1894. Lucy planned to attend, along with her whole family, what promised to be the most important event held thus far in the year-old settlement.[21]

Saturday morning, 1 September 1894, brought no relief from the dry weather that had plagued the Minnesota pineries throughout the long summer. The cool night gave way to a day that showed every promise of being another in a succession of hot ones. With no sign of rain, the long drought went on without letup. The fresh smell of pine needles had long since ceased to permeate the woods. Early risers had expected no change in the weather; none occurred. A light, warm wind blew out of the southwest, carrying a pall of blue-grey smoke that provided a low cloud cover across the region. At intervals the sun shone through, bathing the land in a pale-yellow light that looked as if it came through a diffused filter. Slowly the kaleidoscope changed, first to a deep black and then back to blue-grey.

People throughout the area noticed the strange coloring in the sky, but most rationalized it and blamed it on the wind. After all, fires had burned all summer in the bush. There was no danger. The smoke came from stumps that smouldered to life under certain weather conditions. Life would go on as before. The rains would eventually come, no need to worry about the strange colors in the sky. They would provide a good subject for conversation during the winter months when people would tell tales about the "drought of '94," and how it could have resulted in dreadful fires that would have destroyed thousands of square miles of timber and killed hundreds of people. January hot-stove sessions lent themselves to tall stories about the north woods. With below zero temperatures and several feet of snow covering the ground, the clouds of the black September would have only abstract importance.

No one cried wolf on 1 September. It was difficult to tell the source of the smoke. It might have been dozens of miles away. Dr. C. A. Kelsey of Pokegama summed matters up: "It would be interesting to call attention to the fact that on a clear day a fire that is a long distance off appears to be very near. When the fires first began, they were burning all around the country. I was greatly alarmed one day by a fire which appeared to be very near us, but upon investigation proved to be about six miles away. The day of the great fire the atmosphere was filled with smoke, but none were aware of their danger until it was upon them. The question among the people was 'Is there danger?' One was running to another asking, 'Where is the fire?' and no one seemed to be able to answer the question."[22]

Normal activities characterized the morning hours. In Hinckley the mill workers prepared for a ten-hour shift. They climbed out of bed, washed, dressed, breakfasted, and walked to work. The vast majority looked forward to receiving their pay envelopes and spending Saturday night on the town. Some probably winced as they contemplated the extent of their hangovers the morning after. Original sin abounded in a lumber town, despite the statutes of the state of Minnesota. A few men probably flexed their muscles and clenched their fists, looking ahead to a drunken brawl. It would make for a satisfying evening.

Other sights and sounds broke the stillness of the September morning. In Miller, several miles north of Hinckley on the St. Paul & Duluth, many of the adults and children prepared to harvest potatoes, the sole crop that seemed to grow well among the pine stumps. It was exacting and hard work. Three miles south of Hinckley at Mission Creek on the same railroad haying was the order of the day. To those involved the weather actually seemed a blessing: the hay needed harvesting before the fall rains. At the Minnesota Trust Company quarries in Sandstone on the Eastern Minnesota nine miles north of Hinckley, employees reported for work. Peter Peterson, the superintendent, gave little thought to the smoke drifting overhead. He worried that the weather might change and force a temporary work stoppage; the possibility of a forest fire never crossed his mind.[23]

At Duluth-Superior railroad workers started to make up the two limited trains scheduled to make the run down to the Twin Cities. Yard employees of the Eastern Minnesota also prepared freight train No. 23. It would steam south to Hinckley from West Superior at 7:00 a.m. and return. With all the switching, the familiar sound of cars banging and coupling filled the air. The men labored under a morning sun slightly obscured by a wood-smoke haze. The atmosphere on the banks of Lake Superior was crisp and invigorating, almost always cooler there than in the pineries.

Below Duluth-Superior, other trains were already moving on both the Eastern Minnesota and the St. Paul & Duluth. Two passengers highballed south toward Minneapolis-St. Paul; from the other direction, the morning passenger trains roared north. In addition to the normal flow of freight traffic, C. P. Fadden, the number one engineer in seniority on the line, and fireman N. Reider rode damaged Engine 19 on the St. Paul & Duluth toward the main yards in St. Paul. They left Duluth in mid-morning, expecting to reach Hinckley about 2:00 p.m. On the Eastern Minnesota, at St. Cloud, engineer William Vogel opened the throttle in the engine of accommodation train No. 45 and started toward Hinckley. The seven-man crew looked forward to an easy trip. John Sanderluis, an express messenger for the Great Northern Express Company, recalled, "It was a beautiful clear day, but very warm in the forenoon, and the boys were congratulating themselves on a light day's work."[24]

When Tom Campbell and J. T. Clark woke in the woods at first light, they heard the cry of the loon and the chirping of other birds. As they went about their chores with alacrity, the two looked forward to a day of angling on Lake Eleven, located west of Sandstone. Although the strange coloring in the sky and the smell of wood smoke bothered them, they shrugged it off and concentrated on the day's fishing.[25] They approved of the southwest breeze, stirring up the surface water just enough without making a rowboat drift too rapidly out of the bays. Experience showed that fish usually did not bite well in still water. Of course, neither expected much trouble catching large numbers of northern pike. Three- and four-pounders easily took the casting lure during the last half of the summer. The vicious sharp-toothed fish lurked in the shallow water of every small bay, sometimes back among the weeds. Walleyes were another matter. They tended to stay deep in their holes, usually alongside a reef. The best time to angle for them was early evening or right after a rain squall. It required patience, jerking a line lightly as it bumped along the bottom. The two fishermen had less confidence about netting walleyes than northerns. They would just have to wait and see how things went.

Several miles west of Pokegama a band of Chippewa Indians from the Mille Lacs Reservation had established a hunting lodge along one of the forks of Sadridge Creek. They had been there since early July. The "big chief" of the party, Chief Wacouta, had with him twenty-two followers including men, women, and children. Their camp consisted of Wacouta's tepee, held together with rawhide thongs, plus a half-dozen birchwood shanties. They also had a number of rifles and shotguns. When, on the early afternoon of 1 September, the sky turned completely black and fire seemed all around, Wacouta weighed his options. To stay meant certain death: fire would overrun the camp within a few minutes. To go east seemed illogical. The rapidly rising wind blew that way, and the flames would go in that direction. The best chance seemed a breakout to the west over a trail leading back toward the reservation, about thirty miles away. The chief formed up his people and led them out, not wasting time to gather belongings. The grave situation necessitated the men's leaving behind all their weapons.[26] Prospects appeared bleak, but Wacouta had been in tough spots before. He had the advantage of knowing the woods and maybe that would get everyone through.

The Red Demon came out of the forest fastness. He advanced with a thunderous roar, accompanied by a massive black cloud of smoke that stretched toward the heavens. He tossed out great bolts of flame. Sometimes his advance guard engulfed victims in clouds of smoke so that he entrapped them before they knew what happened. At others, he pushed ahead walls of heat, killing in advance of his arrival. He toyed with his prey, slowly closing in upon them or rushing along, running over them and turning them into cinders within seconds. Nothing could stop the black and red monster after the unleashing of his full fury. Many fires seeking air created him. At least one had led the way, pushing through layers of hot air, reaching the cold above and creating an updraft. Once the flames of many merged into one, the demon stalked the woodlands, pushed on by a rising wind and by those of his own fury. He would roll along, unstoppable, destroying everything he touched. He would ignite huge trees in a flash, or he would feed on the dry slashings in the underbrush. He would jump streams and cunningly feel his way around lakes. A murderer. Those fortunate enough to escape his wrath came away with indelible impressions. A survivor of a visitation recalled, "The dense columns of smoke now rolling majestically upwards, now torn and riven by the wind into fantastic forms and black as midnight, now flaming red and in a moment gone, leaving in its place a vacuum as transparent as space, now deafening the ear with its roar; now still as death and again seething, crackling, hissing, sounding at one time like the roll of distant thunder, or the ocean surf trampling on the sea shore, and again lapsing into death-like silence."[27]

Chapter 2

"Escape for Your Lives.
Hinckley Will Be Destroyed!"

By noon on 1 September 1894, people in Pine County started to worry. They could no longer ignore the menacing smoke and cinders. A homesteader, Gustave Wenz, a "phlegmatic Teuton," decided to leave his farm before it was too late. Loading his family and a few belongings into a wagon, he hitched up a team of "faithful horses" and drove the short distance to Hinckley. All along the way he saw burning stumps. This was enough to send him back into the country to bring in a neighboring family. After that he made still another trip into the woodlands to rescue friends on a remote farm.[1]

In Hinckley a large fire burning in the marsh land to the west of the Brennan Lumber Company caused crews to work all morning trying to contain the blaze. J. W. Stockholm, one of the men detailed to support the fire fighting, supplied empty barrels used to haul water. "It was burning very badly in the west part of town all the forenoon in the swamps," he said. While things looked "pretty bad," he "did not think things serious."[2]

Douglas Greeley, the proprietor of the Morrison Hotel and the county auditor, watched things get steadily worse. "September 1st, at noon, it began to look scarey; in the south, toward Mission Creek, it looked bad," he recalled. "There was a very hot smoke densely black, and a light wind." He became so concerned that he sent his family away on the midday train from Duluth to St. Paul. It arrived over an hour late at about 2:00 p.m., slowed by heavy smoke blowing over the line. After the passenger train pulled out, Greeley walked south several times to look down the Eastern Minnesota tracks. Conditions became progressively poorer, the sky growing darker by the minute, until suddenly the sun broke through the cover. At that moment, Greeley stood in front of his hotel talking to William Ginden, a former mayor of Hinckley and a current member of the county board of supervisors. Ginden's teenage son appeared and asked, "Father, do you want mother to leave home and seek a place of safety? She wants to know." After intently studying the clearing sky, the older man replied quietly, "Willie, run home and tell mama the danger is past."[3]

Down the track in Mission Creek the inhabitants were not so sure. "The light breeze blowing in the morning grew stronger as the hours went by until at twelve o'clock a hurricane was bearing down upon us from the direction of the fire," a Mission Creek resident remembered. "A solid mass of dry pine clippings and underbrush, augmented here and there with a few hundred tons of hay, furnished ample food for the hungry hell which was approaching."[4] By 2:00 p.m. the wind howled with unrelenting fury. All the seventy-three people gathered at the log building that served as a combination store, railroad station, and telegraph office. Normally, there would have been more, but the Laird & Boyle sawmill had been sold and permanently closed a month earlier. Plans called for dismantling the machinery and shipping it to Arkansas. Many of the former employees had left for North Dakota to help with the wheat harvest. There was much confusion and some persons shouted at the mill manager, Joseph Boyle, telling him to summon a train. He calmed the fears by forcefully pointing out that Mission Creek's thirty buildings and the mill, all owned by Laird & Boyle, stood in a wide clearing. Hence, they need not panic. There was little chance of a fire destroying Mission Creek.[5]

At Pokegama the 130 people in the area viewed the sky with increasing alarm. Early in the afternoon many families gathered together in their homes; no one really knew what else to do. Dr. C. A. Kelsey explained, "My own family, a short time before the fire, was scattered, one little boy having gone to the store and another unloading lath; but a few minutes before the fire came, we were all together in our home."[6] Lucy Kelsey's husband returned just before 2:00 p.m.; he and his oldest son had put roughly twenty dollars worth of lumber in water for protection against fire damage. Right after they reached the cabin the wind increased and tore through the open windows, bending the stems on the house plants and causing the curtains to stand straight out. Maidie, the oldest daughter, cried out in fear and wandered aimlessly around the living room. Lucy, efficient as ever, prepared for the worst. She wrote, "I took a little basket, used as a lunch bucket, and going to the bureau took out my gold watch, pocket book, my glasses, new and carefully fitted to my eyes a few weeks before in the city, looked for some valuable papers, and put in some clean pocket handkerchiefs." Giving Maidie something to do in order to take her mind off the fire, Lucy had her gather together a bundle of clothing, telling her, "If the fire comes this way we must have some of the children's clothing bundled up." Ignoring her husband's advice to stay in the cabin, Lucy hung the basket under her arm and put on a hat. She started to the west along the evergreen path to look for a possible escape route, but after a short distance, she decided to return home. "I began to realize that the smoke was filling these woods," Lucy declared. "As I turned to go back, I saw a squirrel run back and forth as if uncertain which way to go, and noticed that the air was strangely still and that leaves were dropping noiselessly."[7]

The fire swept through Pokegama with startling suddenness shortly after 2:00 p.m. About thirty people in the main settlement ran as fast as they could to a small pond near the railroad bridge, just below the log dam's sluice gates, Mrs. Charles W. Collier carrying a three-week-old baby. The small expanse of water dipped to about fifteen feet in the center. At first the small group stood near the shore. Then the fire ignited the bridge and a large pile of edgings by the dam. The terrified persons in the pond reacted as best they could in the face of the intense heat. They huddled together, ducked beneath the surface, threw water over each other, and when the heat became unbearable, they left only their mouths and nostrils exposed. This afforded only temporary relief: they were all in danger of being boiled alive. Buildings all around exploded into flame: the sawmill, the rooming house, the store, and the houses. The proud symbol of the community, the new school, burned fiercely and collapsed in blackened ruins.[8]

Those unable to reach the pond immediately fared as best they could. Jakey Braman and his father were hauling hay just north of Pokegama. When the flames suddenly approached, the father cried out, "The fire is upon us; the hay will soon be ablaze. Let us leave the horses and wagon and escape for our lives!" The son replied, "Father, you go; I can make a place of safety; you look out for yourself." With no time for discussion, the father leaped from the wagon and ran to the pond by the railroad bridge, diving in just ahead of the flames. Jakey turned the wagon away from the fire. Soon he realized the hopelessness of the situation, reined up, unhitched the horses, and awaited his fate.[9]

Three miles away Mrs. Braman was gathering cranberries with Mr. and Mrs. Joseph Frame and their six children. When the dense smoke came, Joe Frame decided to stay and protect a hay field while the rest of the group started toward town. After the rapidly advancing fire cut them off, they temporarily sought refuge in an old cellar only to be driven out by the sweltering heat. They found a small creek and lay down in the water. Joe Frame soon saw the futility of protecting his hay, ran into the center of a field burned over in a previous fire, and threw himself down in the blackened grass.[10]

Just before the full fury of the fire hit Pokegama, Dr. Kelsey and three other men, John Gonyea, Joe Chipris, and M. C. Anderson, had hurried a mile and a half north of the village to try to help Charles Collier save his home. They felt relatively safe because of the proximity of a large potato patch. A wall of heat drove them to cover on the east side of the building. Next, the entire structure exploded into flame. Dr. Kelsey vividly remembered what happened in the next few minutes: "We jumped into tubs of water, filled our shoes, wet our clothing, and made a dash, during the first ten rods of which, the heat was so intense that it seemed almost impossible for us to breathe and live to get through it. . . . The road led through the green tamaracks, which we felt certain would not burn, but upon reaching them, we found to our horror that they were in flames. Trees had fallen across our road, through the burning tops of which we were obliged to clamor as fast as we could."[11] The men scrambled, stumbled, and staggered to a creek bed. Dr. Kelsey, Chipris, and Anderson fell exhausted into the water, seeking relief from the smoke and flames. Gonyea and Collier continued onward, making their way through an almost-continuous line of fire. Gonyea tired, rolled into a small pool of water, and hunkered down. Collier sprinted ahead, his chest heaving and his side aching. He reached the mill pond and dived in, reunited with his wife and baby.

John Powers, William Thompson, and Frank Lepengraver

busily cut hay about two miles from the settlement. When the fire came, they sought safety in the middle of a meadow. They set a backfire and covered up in wet horse blankets. Powers withstood the heat long enough to throw wet blankets over the heads of his two horses.[12]

Two little sisters on a cranberry-picking expedition a couple of miles south of town heard an ominous roar that sounded like a sudden storm. Realizing it was a fire, they ran to the railroad tracks, tripping and falling in the thick underbrush, dropping their berries and helping each other along. Reaching the railroad, they half filled a bucket with brackish water from a culvert and huddled together in a slight depression, protected by the roots of an old tree. They dipped their aprons in the bucket and held them over their faces, fighting off the suffocating heat. Through the billowing smoke they saw forest creatures seeking safety. "It was a terrible thing to see the little animals of the forest running past, darting here and there, their little hearts pounding, breathless, panicky, many of them with their fur already ablaze," one of the sisters recalled. "Rabbits, deer, chipmunks, all of them were too terror-stricken to be afraid of the two of us, cowering in fear of our lives, too. One little fawn came dashing up to us, paused a moment and with eyes unseeing in terror, dashed off again. A sparrow came up to our feet, tried to fly away, but fell over dead right in front of our eyes."[13]

Throughout the Pokegama area, people made split-second decisions in the face of a roaring inferno. Farmer Thomas Raymond and his wife, both age thirty-five, collected their four children and set off toward the northeast. Fred Molander, another farmer, jumped down his well. His wife stayed in the house, comforting her one- and three-year-old children. Mr. and Mrs. Charles Anderson, along with their daughter and two sons, elected to remain in their cabin. Two miles south of Pokegama, two brothers, both single, took opposite courses: thirty-five-year-old James Barnes decided to fight the fire when it struck their cabin; Robert Barnes, ten years younger, started along a wagon road. Pokegama resident Albert Whitney, thirty years old and married, wandered down the Eastern Minnesota tracks.[14]

☆　　☆　　☆

The Kelseys decided that their only hope was to climb down their well, which had approximately four feet of water in the bottom. They took some blankets along. Their kitten refused to go and vanished into the woods. Rabbits flocked around the well, hopping back and forth with no apparent purpose. "Oh, the poor little rabbits!" exclaimed Lyle, the youngest son. The protruding ladder prevented them from closing the top hatch. As the Kelsey family stood in the water at the bottom of the dark hole, sparks, ashes, and cinders dropped "in showers." Maidie moaned, "Oh, my head, my head."

As the fire roared, Lucy and her children softly sang a hymn:

> Jesus loves me, he who died,
> Heaven's gates to open wide;
> He will wash away my sin,
> Let his little children come in.[15]

The fire continued to howl with unabated fury.

About the time the Red Demon reached Pokegama, the Eastern Minnesota accommodation train from St. Cloud rattled into Hinckley, over two hours late. As fierce and wild black clouds rolled overhead, a small blaze flared in the rear of the Eastern Minnesota roundhouse, occupying the attention of the yard workers. The train crew decided not to wait and did their own switching. They uncoupled some boxcars, swung the locomotive and tender around on the turntable, coupled on a baggage car and coach and adjusted the air brakes. Two passengers climbed aboard, an elderly Pokegama resident and the advance agent for a theatrical company. Instead of the traditional "All aboard," conductor Edward Parr shouted, "Get out of town!" With a jerk, the train started down the tracks, the crew hoping the very light train would make a quick return run to St. Cloud. William Vogel, one of the youngest engineers working on the railroad, intended to open the throttle. He was just starting to get up a good head of steam three miles out of Hinckley when he suddenly applied the brakes and screeched to a halt before the burning Mission Creek bridge, shaking up the people in the cars. After deciding that the rails remained straight, he started over the structure. It sagged as the train crossed without incident. Vogel gave no thought to turning back, even though he realized that terrible things were happening up ahead. He felt that he had no choice except to go forward into the fire storm. The satanic flames were obviously coming right at him at a faster speed than he could reverse. If he backed up he also risked being back-ended by the southbound limited, due in Hinckley at 3:25 p.m. Many people could be killed or maimed. So, Vogel chugged slowly and blindly on into the black smoke, literally feeling his way. The cars shook and rolled, bumping over crooked rails bent by the waves of heat. Two miles from Pokegama, the train jumped the widening tracks. All on board received a bad jolt, but they came through the accident unhurt. No one could tell in the first seconds after the crash what was going on. In the baggage car, John Sanderluis, the express messenger, turned to conductor Parr and cried out, "I guess we are done for now!" Parr looked at him and in a sad and quiet voice acknowledged, "I guess so."

The two men decided that their best hope was to dig holes in the ground and cover themselves. They grabbed shovels and slid open the door, but hot air and flames drove them back, singeing their hands and faces. They ran back to the coach, where Sanderluis reported: "The wind was now blowing a hurricane and the flames were shooting in through every crack and crevice on the coach around the windows and doors. The cushions on the coach then caught fire, and we had to throw them out to keep the fire from spreading. The flames were getting much worse and we gave up all hopes of getting out of there alive. We all laid on the floor to avoid, as much as possible, the heat that came from the windows, and were trying to settle our accounts with our Maker while we had time. But fortune favored us again, when brakeman Whalen thought of the water in the engine tank, and called for volunteers to help him save the coaches which were on fire underneath. Of course everyone was glad to do what they could to save themselves, so we got a couple of pails and started at it in a novel but safe way, two going out at a time and throwing a pail full of water on the fire, then struggling in again, when two more would take their places. After an hour's hard fight, we at last got control of the fire under the cars. While this hard fight for life was going on, the conductor went to see if the engineer and firemen were alive. He found that they were . . . lying on the deck of the engine with the water of the tank turned on them."[16]

At half past two the southbound St. Paul & Duluth passenger train rolled through Mission Creek, with no one making an effort to flag it down. By then, none of the inhabitants felt the situation serious enough to leave, or at least they appeared that way outwardly. They gathered outside the station and watched the train hurry down the track. About half a mile out of Mission Creek it ran into brilliant sunshine, the passengers breathing a sigh of relief. The crew relaxed and concentrated on the intricacies of making up as much time as possible on the remainder of the run down to St. Paul. They had left the fire district and had no idea what horrors lay only minutes behind.

In Mission Creek the fire arrived just after 2:30 p.m., burning all the buildings within minutes. The clearing proved no barrier to the sweep of flames. Pokegama was first; Mission Creek came next. Joseph Boyle, the mill manager who had previously discounted the threat, acted decisively. He told the people to follow him into a potato field to the rear of the station, ordering a couple of men to bring along barrels of water. "Some wanted to start to Hinckley, and did so, but only went a few rods and then returned to the potato patch, where we lay fully two hours with our faces to the ground, until the worst was over," a survivor stated. "The heat was intense and the children were all crying from the heat and ashes that nearly blinded us."[17] The frightened people lay flat against the ground.

By mid-afternoon the residents of Hinckley clearly realized that a great fire raged in the distance. No one had time to contemplate what might have happened in Pokegama and Mission Creek. The immediate concern was to save the town. The sun had vanished again behind the clouds of smoke, as a steady stream of ashes carried by the rising wind fell from above. G. I. Albricht, the bookkeeper at the lumber company, had long since given up trying to concentrate on financial calculations. Although he had sent his wife and two children away to St. Paul as a precautionary measure, deep down he continued to believe that no real danger existed. He wandered the streets waiting for the danger to pass. "Three years ago there was talk about the possible burning of Hinckley," he asserted, "but all the summer of 1894 I never thought it possible that Hinckley would ever burn up, and not until after 3 p.m., on Saturday, September 1st, did I think for an instant that the town would go." He looked south and saw a horrible-looking black cloud bearing down on the village. He declared, "The air grew hotter and drier every moment. The smoke was by this time being driven by the wind."[18] Sooner than most he saw that the town was doomed.

Just after noon, John Craig, chief of the Hinckley Fire Department, had rung a gong that summoned a group of veteran volunteer firemen to the firehouse for a planning session designed to draw up contingency arrangements. "It looks threatening in the south and in the southwest," the chief stated. "I do not think that there is any danger, but it is well to be prepared for an emergency."[19] After a short discussion, the group reached a consensus. They agreed that if a large fire struck it would probably come up the St. Paul & Duluth Railroad from Mission Creek, crossing the Eastern Minnesota Railway, and then attacking the built-up sections of Hinckley. The chief said that he would plan accordingly and adjourned the meeting. So, when he ordered the mill whistle to sound a general alarm at 2:15 p.m., everything was in readiness.

Over 200 men trotted to the fire line. Almost all were seasoned sawmill workers and lumberjacks who understood the woods and knew their jobs. More importantly, they had faith in their organization and leadership. They hoped to deflect the fire around Hinckley, a tough fight, but no one expected to fail. "We had 2,000 feet of hose," Chief Craig said. "At that time we never dreamed that the town would burn."[20] Within a short time, the fire, arriving on a much wider front than expected, forced an extension of the line. It soon stretched from where the tracks crossed the lumberyard around most of the lower west side. By then workers at the lumber company, plus most of the other adults, had joined the fight against the dread monster. While several small structures burned on the western outskirts, sparks and cinders set ablaze a building on the east side. The chief, careful not to show panic, mounted a horse and cantered across town to check. On the way he stopped at the telegraph office to wire Rush City for more hose, still expecting to stop the flames. Obviously, he would not have asked for more equipment if he thought the situation hopeless.

Standing beside Engine 19 on a St. Paul & Duluth siding in Hinckley, a couple of hundred feet from the fire line, engineer C. P. Fadden and fireman N. Reider watched the activity with frustration. They were in a quandary. Railroad regulations stipulated that they remain with the locomotive; they could not help fight the fire. Although they wanted to leave, they had received no orders to either proceed south or go back north. Until then, they had to sit in the yards with nothing to do but wait. They talked quietly, deciding what to do if the flames threatened Engine 19.[21]

Eastern Minnesota freight train No. 23 chugged into Hinckley at 2:45 p.m. with engineer Edward Barry at the controls of Engine 105. The powerful four-wheeler pulled thirty empty and ten full boxcars. The trip south from West Superior had taken eight hours, much longer than expected. Seventeen miles from Hinckley, at Partridge, when the sky had darkened, Barry stopped to light the headlight on the engine, along with those in the cab. From there on, fires burned all along the roadbed and blowing smoke covered the tracks. Barry proceeded very slowly, carefully checking the numerous bridges before crossing. At Sandstone, which No. 23 reached at 2:00 p.m., the extreme darkness made it difficult for the crew to switch cars. Great clouds of black smoke drifting over the train on the nine-mile run from Sandstone prevented brakeman C. C. Freeman from seeing more than half the cars from his post in the caboose. By the time the freight chugged into the Hinckley yards, a disaster seemed in the making, fire threatening the town from all sides. Engineer Barry wrote, "We set out our train on the side track, and went to the lower end of the yard. Everything was on fire, the ties under the rails were burning, and the box cars on the side track were on fire. I got back to the water tank as quickly as I could, it being impossible to see, and the rails started to warp in the yard."[22]

Brakeman Freeman, trying to go about his normal duties,

started to record the numbers on the boxcars for freight train No. 24, the freight's official designation for the return trip. Freeman recorded the necessary information for thirty-four loads. After he wrote down the figures for the thirty-fifth car, he heard two whistles, the signal that the boxcars from the north had been dropped off. As he looked up, the cars right in front of him exploded into flames. When he saw more fire below, where the tracks crossed in the lower yards, he ran back to the station office, taking temporary shelter. The telegraph operator and ticket agent were the only railroad men there: all the rest had gone off to fight the fire.

Meanwhile, Barry and his fireman, A. R. Thistle, decided it was impossible to go down to the turntable by the Eastern Minnesota roundhouse south of the junction to turn Engine 105 and the tender around. So, after backing down the main line, they went forward onto a side track, still facing south. The conductor, W. D. Campbell, walked down the siding, looking with interest at three empty boxcars and a caboose. Recognizing the obvious, he started to plan his next move. In charge of No. 24, he was shortly going to have to make some life and death decisions. "The residents and fire department were out fighting the fire when we arrived, but the heat was so intense and the smoke so blinding that the people were powerless," he stated. "We could not leave Hinckley as the wires were down and train No. 4 was due there at 3:25 p.m."[23]

Fast passenger train No. 4 on the Eastern Minnesota thundered south into the holocaust. Veteran engineer William Best had hold of the throttle of Engine 125, a four-wheeler, while his fireman, George Ford, stoked coal into the boiler. Back in the five swaying coaches, crowded with about 125 passengers, conductor H. D. Powers went about normal railroad business, validating tickets, checking seat locations, and answering questions. Powers frequently glanced at his watch. The train had left Duluth on time at 1:00 p.m., and he hoped to remain on schedule all the way to St. Paul, despite the fires in the woods. "On the way to Hinckley we didn't see any more fire than we had seen every day for weeks before," Powers recalled, "but over part of the distance, the smoke was very thick and it was so dark we were obliged to use our lanterns and the engineer lighted his headlights."[24] At the long Kettle River bridge, two miles above Sandstone, the watchmen had trouble seeing the numbers on the train's side as it slowed to the mandatory four miles an hour and then gained speed, moving toward the south.[25] The train crew expected to leave the smoke. They knew from past runs that the air usually cleared in the open territory south of Sandstone.

Riders in the coaches worried about the smoke and flames swirling past the windows, while George S. Cole, the news agent, tried to reassure them. "All went well until we got close to Dedham, Wisconsin, which is about fifteen miles from Duluth, and then we discovered the woods on fire, and the atmosphere in the cars became hot and smoky," he explained. "In passing through the cars, back and forth, I was questioned by many of the passengers as to the probable danger from the fire, and I informed them that I apprehended no danger after the train got out of the woods."

Up in the locomotive cab, engineer Best saw Hinckley as No. 4 swung around a gentle curve. He was both apprehensive and optimistic about what lay ahead: "The air did appear to clear somewhat, but the clouds seemed to be on fire, and great sheets of flame athwart the heavens with electrical activity. When we came in view of Hinckley everything was quiet except the southern extremity of town, and in the Great Northern yards, where the fire had made its appearance."[26] He slowed the heavy train, arriving in Hinckley on time, exactly at 3:25 p.m.

Just as No. 4 slowed to a crawl, buildings throughout Hinckley burst into flames and the fire line collapsed. The fire, according to an eyewitness, "came galloping in great leaps, like froth on the greatest billows of the stormy ocean, and with a speed as if it were eager to seize everthing that was fleeing before it, later to settle down to a steadier pace and lick its way forward as if in playfulness."[27] Father E. J. Lawler, a Roman Catholic priest and a well-known figure in the community and in the volunteer fire department, became the first fire fighter to abandon the hopeless struggle. Either out of justifiable fear or because of a clear perception of the danger from houses burning in the rear of the fire line, he suddenly ran, shouting at the top

of his lungs, "Escape for your lives. Hinckley will be destroyed!"
He came upon a large number of people hitching teams to
wagons laden with household belongings. "For heaven's sake,
leave all you have!" he exclaimed. "Get to the gravel pit, run
to the river! Hinckley will be destroyed!" A man turned and
snarled at the priest, "To hell with that sort of advice!" Not
stopping to argue, Father Lawler continued through the streets,
screaming over and over: "The city will be destroyed! Escape
for your lives! Run to the gravel pit; run to the river! Leave
all you have, save your lives!"[28] He sprinted to the Grindstone
River and plunged in, seeking refuge in the cool water.

Chief Craig, after sending the telegram for help to Rush City
and deciding to his own satisfaction that the burning buildings
on the east side posed no immediate danger, rode his horse back
to the fire line. Along the way, men ran by going in the opposite
direction. When Craig reached the front, he found "everybody
gone." His defense had understandably melted away in minutes;
the Red Demon had arrived with his main force. As bolts of
flame rocketed overhead into the heart of Hinckley, all hope
vanished. Chief Craig wheeled his mount and galloped into the
dying city, crying, "We can't save the town; it's burning at the
south end; run to the gravel pit; don't lose a moment, but fly!"
He thought of his wife, mother, and sister; perhaps he could
get them on the passenger train that had just arrived.[29]

Passenger train No. 4 stopped for a minute in front of the
station, and then pulled several hundred feet ahead to the water
tower. When fireman George Ford quickly wrenched down the
water spout to fill Engine 125's tender, three times the intense
heat drove him away. He would have given up except for
engineer Best, who, according to Ford, "called to me in his
always pleasant way to fill the tank if I could." The hot work
took Ford about two minutes. After he finished, Best backed
the passenger train up the track to the station. "We were
standing at the passenger station, and the wind was blowing
a gale," Ford declared. "It was not more than five or ten minutes
before a sheet of flame shot up to the clouds, and the whole
town was on fire."[30]

Panic spread throughout the streets. No one stopped to check the time carefully, but it was probably about 3:30 p.m. The people had only one thing on their minds: to flee for their lives and escape the swirling flames and intense heat. The Reverend Peter Knudsen, the Presbyterian minister in Hinckley, described what happened in the first moments of terror: "The fact is they lost their reason and stampeded like a lot of frightened cattle head-long to destruction. . . . I never saw such a sadder sight. The horrors of the battlefield are nothing in comparison."[31] Men, women, and children milled through the streets as news spread of the fire line's failure. Some persons gathered household goods and family valuables, while others rushed to root cellars or went down wells. Thirteen people leaped into one well. Individuals doused themselves with water, hoping to ward off the intense heat. Yet at this point no known lives had been lost in Hinckley. After the first wave of panic subsided, people gradually regained self-control, overcoming the initial shock that Hinckley would surely burn to the ground.

Most residents were wondering how long they had to escape. Several hundred ran in the general direction of the Eastern Minnesota passenger station. Those whom Father Lawler had warned without success to flee immediately continued to load their wagons, preparatory to leaving town to the north over the old government wagon road. Many of the more than one hundred persons numbered among the poorest in Hinckley. A majority had recently immigrated from Sweden. With nothing beyond their wagons, teams, and personal belongings, they felt no choice except to try to save them. Professional and business leaders also lingered, but for different reasons. Believing that their standing in the community required that they set examples, they collected important records, carrying some with them and placing others in iron safes. Some took their families to the Eastern Minnesota station and then walked back to their establishments, intending to remain as long as possible.[32]

☆   ☆   ☆

Judge Seagrave Smith, a prominent Minneapolis judge, was a passenger on No. 4. His relief on seeing the sun briefly just before the train rolled into Hinckley lasted only until it started to take on water. As he stepped out of a car to watch fireman Ford work at the spout, Smith noted a number of railroad cars burning to the south in the yards. Suddenly, a fierce wind blew hot dust into his face, causing him to turn his head; he jumped back on the train.

Judge Smith, one of the few people aboard trained at accurately observing and evaluating information, six months later composed a careful analytical account of what happened next on the afternoon of the terrible September day. While his observations reflect his legal training, describing conditions without conveying the horror and suffering, they provide an accurate statement of the events between roughly 3:30 and 3:45 p.m. in the vicinity of the Eastern Minnesota station. Judge Smith wrote, "Before we had stopped at the station the people from the village, men, women, and children, came running toward the train with their trunks and bundles. Others were running with their effects and locating themselves in a large and deep gravel pit on the east side of the station, the bottom of which was nearly all covered with shallow water. When the train stopped at the station there was a short consultation between the conductor, myself, and a few others as to what should be done. It was decided best to stay there as long as it would be safe and prudent — get on all the people we could in that time, and get away before the fire should entirely surround us." The judge watched the progress of the conflagration and the people trying to save themselves from destruction. "Many got on the train; others sought for safety in the gravel pit referred to — all frightened," he remembered. "It was a heart-rending sight to behold — the wind was blowing a fearful gale. The flames of fire were leaping high and consuming everything it came in contact with almost instantaneously. I saw on the west side of the village a volume of flame strike a small house and shed, wipe it out in an instant, and leap from there over a number of other buildings without touching them, strike a saw mill beyond with such force that it was moved bodily from its foundations in a second, and went floating in the air a burning mass; every stick of timber in it seemed to be on fire. On turning to the other side, I saw that the fire had burned around the gravel pit and was fast gaining in front of us. The people of the village, during this time, were running in every direction, and getting in the cars or into the gravel pit with such effects as they could carry along with them. I saw one man who carried nothing with him but his gun."[33]

Shortly after No. 4 reversed back to the passenger station, conductors Powers and Campbell held a short conversation. It could have been awkward. Campbell, in work clothes, ran a freight train. Powers, resplendent in his blue uniform that denoted a badge of great authority and distinction in the United States of 1894, had responsibility over a fast limited. However, Eastern Minnesota regulations complicated the situation: they had the force of law and could not be controverted by seniority and privilege. Powers's passenger train No. 4 had no authority to return up the line and all the wires were down. Campbell's freight train No. 24 had a clear line all the way to West Superior. Campbell, who had mulled over his options since he walked down the side track to look at the three empty boxcars and caboose, took the initiative. He already knew what he wanted to do. He suggested to Powers that they solve the legal and administrative problem by creating a combination train, officially designated freight train No. 24. Engineer Barry would take Engine 105, on the side track, farther down the rails and couple up to the empty cars. He would then back up onto the main line, and go forward a short distance, hooking onto the back of No. 4. The resulting train, Barry's Engine No. 105 in front, three freight cars, a caboose, five passenger coaches, and Best's Engine 125 bringing up the rear, would take on as many people as possible before reversing up the line. It would not be an easy trip: both locomotives would be facing south and there were no turntables between Hinckley and Duluth-Superior. After the combination train started, Barry would serve as the engineer and Best as the brakeman. Once a train was underway, the engineer made the decisions; he had the "right of the road." Of course, Campbell would act as the conductor; No. 4 would technically become part of No. 24. Powers, the senior of the two, would remain in overall charge. In any event, the arrangement was practicable from a safety standpoint. If a lead train stopped or jumped the track, a following one might pile into it in the thick smoke.

Powers quickly accepted the proposal, believing it the only proper course of action. While Campbell went over to the side track to give Barry instructions, Powers walked down and asked

Best, "What do you think of putting the freight behind us?" He had brought up exactly what Best wanted to do. "We understood each other without talking much," Best wrote. "The wind was blowing a gale by this time, and we realized that Hinckley was doomed. The people now commenced running from the burning town to the train. In fact, they were running anywhere and everywhere, for they were panic stricken."[34] Best jumped down from the cab and asked Powers how much longer they could stay and still get away. No reply came. The two men stood beside the locomotive and watched people climb into the coaches.

J.W. Stockholm, who had spent the morning helping to fight the fire in the marsh west of the Brennan Lumber Company, had given up and gone to his home, a block west of the Eastern Minnesota gravel pit. He told his wife, three children, two sisters, and sixteen-year-old nephew to have a few barrels of water in readiness to ward off falling cinders. At 3:25 p.m., after noting the arrival of the passenger train, Stockholm walked back to work at the lumber company store, braving blasts of hot air that made it difficult for him to keep his eyes open. At the store he discussed the bleak situation with G. I. Albricht, the bookkeeper, who was already convinced the town would burn. Suddenly, Stockholm's nephew, Hans Hanson, arrived on a bike, reporting that the whole east side was ablaze. Stockholm decided the time had come to "get out." After persuading the widow Resbery and her four children, ages three to nine, who had sought refuge in the store, to accompany him, he went back the approximately 1,200 feet to his home. He found the house empty and fire rolling overhead. He told his nephew to stay and help Mrs. Resbery and her children while he went to the gravel pit to find his family. A friend, Asel Hanson, told him they had started north up the Eastern Minnesota tracks. Stockholm ran down the railroad, found them, and turned them back toward the quarry, a fierce wind blowing cinders in their faces as they struggled down the right-of-way. Stockholm, winded from running, lagged behind. The rest of the family neared the pit just as engineer Barry stopped his freight on the main line, prior to coupling to the passenger. They climbed into the first boxcar and hoped for the best,

Stockholm joining them soon afterwards. Meanwhile, the young nephew, Mrs. Resbery, and her children had all boarded the passenger train.[35]

Bookkeeper Albricht, after leaving the store, ran directly to the residence of Annie Wescott, his wife's sister. When he found her carefully packing valuables, Albricht said, "Annie, leave those things and come along with me, if we save our lives that is all we may expect to do." They hurried to the St. Paul & Duluth station, hoping to take the next train to Pine City. When the fire "appeared to come in a sheet of flame over the town," they "made a rush"[36] across town to the Eastern Minnesota combination train and got aboard.

Attention focused on the Eastern Minnesota train. Some men put their loved ones on the train and then turned back into town, fire chief Craig one of them. Finding his wife, he got her to the station in time to catch the train. Ignoring her pleas, he walked away to look for his mother and sister. John Hogan could not walk because of a hip ailment. His brother drove him to the train, went back for their mother, found her, and got her aboard. But there was no room for him; he remained behind. Paul Licke, the only tailor in Hinckley, saved the lives of two hysterical "young ladies" by picking them up bodily and carrying them to the station, then ran back into the raging fire to try to help any stragglers. Joseph Tew, a drayman and volunteer fireman, managed to find places on the train for his wife and six of his children; then Tew, his oldest daughter, and his mother started north with a team and wagon hauling possessions.[37]

Mayor Lee Webster of Hinckley had fought on the fire line. When it collapsed, he ran home and told his twenty-six-year-old wife, Belle, that the fire was burning out of control. He went to the barn and, after a great deal of trouble, calmed his two horses, hitching them to a wagon. The dense smoke made it difficult to see. Going back to the house, he found his wife had gone and assumed she had fled to the gravel pit. When he arrived there, he could not find her. Webster next thought that she had boarded the train. "The eastern Minnesota train was standing on the track, and I went through several cars, but did not find my wife among the refugees," he said. "As there were several cars it was impossible for me to get through I thought she must be in one of them."[38] Feeling somewhat relieved, he left the train, mounted his rig, and rode into town to see what he could do to help. After passing a team hitched to a wagon without a driver, he found two women and seven children. Getting them on his wagon, he started toward the gravel pit. Mayor Webster could do nothing more to save his town; things were absolutely hopeless.

Kate Barnum, the thirteen-year-old daughter of Dr. E. E. Barnum of Pine City, was visiting friends in Hinckley. The people with whom she was staying decided to leave on the Eastern Minnesota train. After going to the station with them, she made an impulsive decision. She would go across town and catch the St. Paul & Duluth southbound limited, due at 4:05 p.m. By taking that train, she planned to arrive home by the supper hour and set the minds of her parents at ease. She reached the St. Paul & Duluth station just as the mill and lumberyard, across the tracks, burst into flames. She ran back to the Eastern Minnesota train. Then, for an inexplicable reason, she turned and started back across town for a second time where she found the St. Paul & Duluth depot and the railroad bridge over the Grindstone River burning with great fury. Escape to the south seeming impossible, she turned and ran east, but by now she was out of breath. She frequently fell, rose again, and hurried on toward the Eastern Minnesota train. She reached it; people helped her aboard.[39]

Right after freight No. 24 coupled onto passenger No. 4, engineer Barry decided the time had come to get out of Hinckley as quickly as possible. Since his engine was north of the built-up sections of the village, he could not see down the streets. He whistled sharply twice — the signal to pull out. Engineer

Best, standing alongside his locomotive, watched people continue to run toward the train, then he jumped up into the cab and applied the air brakes. "We were loading women and children, and as I had just come over the road, I was determined to stand on my judgment," he explained. "But again and again did the freight engine whistle off brakes, and try to start the train." Conductor Campbell dashed the length of the train and yelled up to Best, who had his hand on the brake, "Barry will cut off his engine and pull out." Best shouted, "I guess not!" A brakeman appeared and said Barry was determined to leave. From the front of the train, the whistle continued to wail.

As if Best did not have enough trouble, four men jumped onto the engine screaming, "Back up! back up! or we will all be burned to death!" One of them was "Bull" Henley, the Eastern Minnesota section foreman in Hinckley. He and the others were not cowards, nor had they lost their self-control. They simply spoke the truth. Best replied, "Boys, do not get excited; we are all right yet!" Seemingly reassured, they climbed off and hurried to help people board the train. Bull Henley asserted his authority and made sure that women and children came first. People remembered him as a tower of strength, but no one ever saw him alive again. By now things were terrible. Best, continuing to apply the brakes, turned to fireman Ford and exclaimed, "Good God! Will I sacrifice the train at last!"[40]

Dr. Ernest L. Stephan, a young physician who had been in Hinckley for only a few months, had stayed in his office since the first alarm, making no effort to see if anyone needed his help. He justified his behavior, stating, "I was in my office until it got so hot it wouldn't hold me. I then went through all the houses in the south part of town to see that no one was left behind. The men were all out fighting the fire and it was women and children that were left. I carried a number of children to the train. I don't know how many. I should think though at least twenty. I went into my office the last thing to get some articles I wanted, and when I opened the door the fire was right upon me, and I closed the door and waited until the first gust had passed, I then ran and got on the Eastern Minnesota train."[41] No eyewitnesses who wrote accounts of the disaster credited Dr. Stephan with such noble service, although they singled out

44

numerous "heroes" with lavish praise. If the physician did check all the houses on the south side and carry twenty children to the station, his feats went unnoticed in the general confusion.

Engineer Best, with a clear view down a Hinckley street, could see into the burning heart of the dying community. Before his eyes, men, women, children, and animals coming toward the train slowed and dropped, then rolled over and lay still. When Best swung halfway down Engine 125's ladder for a better look, a blast of hot wind struck his face. "Houses were burning so rapidly that one could see bedroom sets and other contents of the rooms," he declared. "The fire would seem to burn the sides right off the buildings, revealing the contents in the glare. Buildings seemed to melt rather than burn in the fierce glow." He remounted the cab and, as he released the brake, the train jerked and moved up the line. Best wrote, "We backed rapidly away from this scene of ruin and death, and as we passed the road running north of the station, we saw people running toward the train, and beckoning us to stop. But it was useless to think of it, for they were too far away from us, and I turned my head that I might not see them in their distress."[42] It was about 3:45 p.m., Central Standard Time.

Angus Hay, the editor of the weekly Hinckley *Enterprise*, after watching the fire strike the town's southern environs, had returned to his northside newspaper office. As he and an assistant, James Willard, worked to save a few "articles" in the print shop, large cinders beat against the windows. When women and children started to run by, they gave up, grabbed the *Enterprise* files and the subscription book, and started to the Eastern Minnesota station. In the crowded streets, Hay soon lost sight of his assistant. Hay dropped his records to assist a woman with two children and a baby. Carrying the baby a couple of blocks ahead, he handed it to a man in a horse and buggy, then went back to help the mother with her two other children. They struggled toward the station, arriving there after the train had left, though they could still hear it in the distance. Hay told the mother to take her children and seek safety in the gravel pit, and he then rushed back into Hinckley. The debilitating heat failed to stop him in his effort to get more people out. Passing two crumpled bodies, he continued. In front of the city hall he found two women kneeling in prayer. "With unintentional disrespect," he observed, "I stopped the prayer meeting and started the ladies for the pit."[43] He followed as fast as he could, there being nothing else to do.

A sea of wind and flames had rushed into Hinckley, causing the village to burn like a gigantic torch. A massive convection tower boiled miles into the sky. Horrible things happened. A woman poured a can of kerosene over her head, believing it to be water. When a hot cinder ignited the substance, she exploded in a sheet of flames. People died in their homes, among them former Mayor Ginden, his wife, and two children; less than two hours after Ginden had thought the danger past, his house had become his funeral pyre. The thirteen people who had dived into a single well were all asphyxiated.[44] No one who stayed in Hinckley proper after 3:50 p.m. had any chance of survival, because the entire lower half had been totally destroyed and almost all of the buildings on the north side were in flames.

On the government road the predominantly immigrant caravan of 125 men, women, and children moved north away from Hinckley as fast as possible. Whips cracked over the horses' ears as the wagons rumbled over the eighty-foot-long Grindstone River bridge, about half way between the two railroads. The town lay behind. Ahead was open country. A woman clutched her Swedish Bible.[45]

Douglas Greeley, the keeper of the Morrison Hotel, had to decide what to do about his six "girls." Ida Jana, who "worked" in the dining room, asked, "What shall we do, what shall we do?" He told her, "Stay here till I tell you to leave. You will be all right. I will go out and will tell you presently what is best to do." Walking outside, Greeley looked up and down the

street, returned, and said, "Now is the time to save ourselves."
Greeley did not really care about his women: he left them to
fend for themselves. Instead, thinking of his cows and horses,
he went out the front door of the hotel, turned to the rear, and
ran to the barn, where three employees had started to release
the animals. The group drove three horses and four cows out
into the streets, then two of the men dashed off. One, Albert
Nuderwood, ran toward the Eastern Minnesota tracks. Greeley
and D. Fortin got several more cows out of the barn, with
another man, Charles Nehland, joining in the task. Just as the
barn and hotel caught fire, the horses returned. After hitching
one to a buggy, Nehland rode off in the general direction of
the gravel pit. Greeley and Fortin saddled the other two mounts
and galloped north out of Hinckley, over the Grindstone bridge.
Seeing the train moving up the track, they hastened towards
it. When the horses charged through some willows, Greeley
bellowed, "We are done now." Fortin shouted, "Yes, I guess
we are." They reached the track as the train slowed and stopped.
Nuderwood, who had made the train, beckoned at them from
an open boxcar. The two men leaped from their mounts, ran
the few yards to the car, and eagerly accepted aid to get on
board. Greeley said he never heard "a sound so welcome" as
the call to get on the train. From the boxcar door, he watched
the Brennan Lumber Company's main building collapse in a
shower of sparks.[46]

Engineer Barry had stopped less than a mile from the station
and not long after crossing the Grindstone River. Seeing men,
women, and children coming from all directions, he said, "I
called for brakes and reversed engine, and stopped and picked
up the people and then started again and ran as fast as a wheel
could turn under an engine."[47] He had about 600 persons on
the train.

At the St. Paul & Duluth station, a young telegrapher,
Thomas G. Dunn, hunched over his key, frantically sending
unanswered signals up the line. Above him, the roof burned
fiercely, but he ignored pleas from bystanders on the platform

to leave his post. Intent on carrying out his duties, he believed that hundreds of lives depended upon his actions. Just after 4:00 p.m., the roof collapsed, burying Dunn in the burning wreckage.[48] The horrified onlookers, most of whom had been waiting for the southbound limited due within minutes, turned away from the scene of death and ran north toward the already-flaming railroad bridge over the Grindstone River.

On the siding south of the station, engineer C. P. Fadden and fireman N. Reider, both of whom had waited in vain several hours for orders about what to do with Engine No. 19, watched the station blaze like a torch. Their own predicament was obvious. Not only had they no instructions, but they had no way of knowing the whereabouts of the passenger train. If they could back over the burning bridge and on up the line, they ran the risk of a collision in the billowing smoke. Rather than take that alternative, they followed a plan agreed upon earlier in the afternoon. Opening the throttle, Fadden steamed south through the searing heat into the Eastern Minnesota yards. There, he backed up to a point near the roundhouse, which stood in a relatively open area and which had not yet burst into flame. Correctly calculating that twisted rails precluded any attempt to run south over either the St. Paul & Duluth or the Eastern Minnesota, Fadden and Reider gambled that the worst fury of the forest fire had passed and they settled down to wait. At this late hour, they were the only people in Hinckley to move directly south through the dying town.[49]

Al Fraser of Hinckley had managed to get one of his three children on the Eastern Minnesota combination train. Before he could get his wife and other two children on board, the over-crowded train pulled out. Finding an abandoned team and wagon, Fraser loaded his family, and drove north over the government road. The heat became so intense shortly after they crossed the bridge over the Grindstone River that the wagon caught fire. Jumping to the ground, the group gave up hope of survival. Just then, a providential thing happened. "After we had turned the first team loose, I noticed something coming toward me through the smoke which proved to be another team of horses and wagons which had been abandoned by their owners," Fraser said. "I caught the team and loading the wife and little ones into the wagon drove on. I found four barrels and a trunk on the wagon, and after driving a little way I found that the barrels were full of water. Just think of it, four barrels of water at a time when above all things else water was to be most desired. I put my children right into the barrels, and broke open the trunk, and wetting the clothes I found there I put them round my wife. About that time two Norwegians came along and crawled into two of the barrels that we had used most of the water out of, and so escaped with their lives at least. One other gentleman was also saved by the water which put in its appearance so fortunately."

A short distance up the road the large immigrant party had abandoned their wagons and sought protection in a swale. Usually covered with water, it had dried up completely during the hot summer drought. The men, women, and children struggled toward the middle, where a wall of heat thrown ahead by a tongue of the great conflagration swept over them. Fraser never forgot what he heard. "When that wave struck them one wail of anguish went up from the whole people as one man, and in less than a minute after everything was still except for the roar of the wind and the crackling of the flames," he recalled. "It all came so quickly; an instant all was over."[50] For many other people it was not yet over; the fire rolled on, seeking new victims.

Chapter 3

"For God's Sake Will You Save Us?"

At precisely 1:55 p.m., conductor Thomas Sullivan had swung his lantern and yelled, "All aboard!" Within seconds, passenger train No. 4 of the St. Paul & Duluth Railroad had shuddered and jerked its way out of the Duluth depot, starting its fast run down to St. Paul. In front, four drive wheels turned on Engine 69, which pulled a combination car, a coach, and two chair cars. As the 125 passengers sat back, contemplating the trip south through the fire district, black porter John Blair ministered to the needs of those in his chair car. In the cab, fireman John McGowan stoked the boiler.

James Root, a senior engineer of the St. Paul & Duluth, manned the throttle. A writer described him as "a modest appearing man, a little above the medium height, with an open, honest face, and a general bearing that would convey to a careful observer the impression that he was not a mere carpet knight, but one of sterling worth who could and would understand and do without flinching any duty that might be placed upon him."[1] Born in Greenbush, New York, in 1843, Root had worked on the railroad since he was fourteen years old. During the Civil War he operated the train that served as William T. Sherman's headquarters during the March to the Sea, later running a hospital train that carried sick and wounded Union prisoners away from Andersonville prison. After being mustered out of service, Root moved to Minnesota, married, and worked in lumber mills. Joining the then-new St. Paul & Duluth in 1870 as the engine dispatcher, a year later he became an engineer. Over the next two decades only a few minor accidents marred his record. He had never lost a train — a major feat given the thousands of passengers and railroad workers killed and injured yearly in the Gilded Age of American rails.[2] By 1894 with a satisfactory and meritorious career behind him, Root had certainly earned the right and responsibility to engineer a crack passenger.

Root's train left the station on a hot and sultry afternoon. The haze in the yards gave way to an obvious smoke cover as the engine and the four coaches thundered southward. Remarking that a storm seemed in the offing, Root ordered fireman McGowan to turn on the headlight at Carlton, twenty miles out, where twenty-five passengers boarded. A few miles later, Root lit the cab lamp so he could see the water glass, while back in the coaches the porter turned on the gas lights. The train crew — used to passing through the forest fires — remained calm and assured. The passengers did not share the feelings.

As the train moved down the line and as flames appeared from within the swirling black smoke, many people on No. 4 grew apprehensive and fearful for their lives. L. S. Meeker of the Richmond Grain Cleaning Company noted, "At 3 o'clock we had reached a smoky atmosphere, and by 3:30 the sky was as dark as midnight. The wind was blowing a gale, carrying smoke and charred cinders, and occasionally a fire spot was passed." Another passenger, R. L. Gorman, thought it "as dark as the blackest winter night." A lawyer, C. D. O'Brien, observed "great clouds on both sides of the road" that gradually increased "to render objects almost indistinguishable." He thought that electric lights burning in mills passed along the way added to the "gloom." An official of Crane, Ordway & Co., of Duluth, William H. Blades, remembered that the train moved into "a sort of unnatural twilight with cinders falling through like black smoke" and that "the air became overheated as if blasts from a hot oven were blowing spasmodically." George C. Dunlap of St. Paul claimed that "signs of disaster became apparent" after the limited left Carlton. He said: "The heat grew more intense, the black smoke thickened, until at three o'clock day changed to night and it was necessary to light lamps and headlight. Breathing became more difficult every moment and the danger of suffocating seemed imminent. On we went, running at lightning speed, hoping to pierce the almost impenetrable gloom. As town after town was passed in quick succession, the anxious inhabitants were seen collected in small groups, and evidently much alarmed. Soon a bright red illuminated the heavens. The black forms of trees became blazing firebrands. Then followed the crash of falling timber and the accompanying shower of sparks."[3] As the train chugged up Hinckley Big Hill, the sun appeared and passengers gasped a collective sigh of relief; the fires were local and everything would soon be all right.

When No. 4 reached the top of the incline at 4:05 p.m., engineer Root, peering down the line, saw an astonishing sight. A couple of hundred people streamed toward the train, coming out of Hinckley, less than a mile away. Root yelled across the cab at fireman McGowan, "There must be something wrong at Hinckley." After he released the throttle, Root applied the air brake, stopped the train, and climbed off the engine. He believed it impossible to proceed without running down many of the fleeing refugees. Still, he did not perceive the cause of the danger, the air being relatively free of smoke. An elderly woman and her two daughters reached the engine first. When Root asked the trouble, the only reply he received was, "For God's sake will you save us?" After telling them to board the train, he then watched in bewilderment as dozens more people kept running past to climb on the coaches. B. C. Bartlett, the proprietor of the Eating House, and his wife were among the last to come up the tracks. Root asked the restaurateur what was wrong, and Bartlett replied, "Jim, everybody is burned out and everything is burning at Hinckley." He said that the depot, the water tank, and the bridge were all aflame. After telling him and his wife to get on the train, the veteran engineer contemplated what to do next — wait for more people or back up the train.[4] Counting those from the stricken town, about 300 persons had climbed on board, more than thirty of whom crowded the open vestibules and the car steps.

Root held a hasty conversation with conductor Sullivan; both later gave different accounts of what transpired. Root positively believed he told Sullivan, "I am going back to Skunk Lake," and that when the conductor replied, "We will never get there alive," he retorted, "Then we will die together."[5] Sullivan held equal convictions about the correctness of his version. He wrote, "I said to my engineer, 'Jim, we cannot stay here long, we will have to go back to a place of safety.' Looking around we could see people coming from all directions making for the train, and to the best of my knowledge I received in the neighborhood of one hundred and fifty or one hundred and sixty men, women and children. Thinking all safely on board the train, I was about to signal to start back, when screams to my right attracted my attention. It proved to be a mother and her three little children running for their lives, and the flames grasping like a demon behind them. Those were the last people I loaded on my train.

I then sprang into the first class coach and gave the engineer the bell twice, and the third pull felt to me as though the bell cord were burned off. I ran into the smoking car and gave the bell cord one more pull and we started back."[6] Whatever the merits of either recollection, time did not permit reflective decision making.

C. D. O'Brien had watched men and women who were "seemingly entirely demented and crazed by fear" tear through the barbed-wire fencing along the right-of-way with their bare hands and, equally appalling, throw children across. "Not having seen any fire, this condition of things was unintelligible to most of the passengers," he stated. "For myself, I stepped out upon the platform and down to the ground on the left side of the train, and while the sky was reasonably clear in front it was suffocatingly hot and the ground appeared to be very much heated. Just as I stepped back upon the platform I heard a roar as of a cyclone or tornado, and the trees upon the west side of the track were bent and twisted as though by the beginning of a cyclone which apparently came from the southwest. I stepped across to the other side of the train and looked towards the southwest, when a sudden blast of hot air struck the car, requiring the closing of the door. After it passed I stepped out again and just as I did so ascertained that the roar was caused, not by a cyclone of wind (although the wind was blowing very heavily), but by a burning cyclone, or mountain of bright flame which was rolling up from the Grindstone River directly upon the train."[7]

While O'Brien did not realize it at the time, he was witnessing a phenomenon seen and survived by few human beings — a massive fire storm sweeping out of the southwest at sixty or seventy miles an hour, roaring over ground already devasted by the Red Demon. After gradually turning north, the massive cloud of fire came directly down the St. Paul & Duluth tracks. It literally leaped along, staying on the earth for a time, and then leaving the ground, jumping along to a new location. Eventually, it would vanish into the atmosphere, but it touched down just north of the Grindstone River, creating what one of O'Brien's fellow passengers called a "huge mountain of flame."[8]

William Blades had left his coach to observe the people stream out of Hinckley toward the train. When he asked the first arrivals what was wrong, they screamed that the town was "burning up" and that flames had come "from every direction."[9] When Blades saw the wooden undercarriages of the cars start to burn in spots splattered with axle grease, he briefly considered making a dash for the Grindstone River and throwing himself into the water. However, when Sullivan sounded "All aboard," Blades instinctively swung back onto No. 4.

James Root had just taken his seat and started to reverse the train when the wind suddenly rose. Looking down the line toward Hinckley, he saw at the bridge a cloud of what he believed to be smoke or dust. Things happened very fast after that. Before he finished opening the throttle, an explosion rocked the cab, the window burst, and glass particles tore into his neck and forehead. "The left side of my head and face were pretty well cut up, although I didn't feel anything the worse," he remembered. "The cut in my neck bled a great deal — pretty much all the blood in my body, I should think." Fireman McGowan noticed the wounds, but he did not believe them serious enough to warrant immediate attention. Instead, leaving his post, he ran back and scrambled through the tender's water hole.

As the train started to move backward over the crest of Hinckley Big Hill, Root heard loud yells for help and saw three men running up the track toward the train. After shutting off the engine and applying the air, Root suddenly had second thoughts and mused, "If I stop the windlass it will stop the train and we shall be burned alive."[10] After he reluctantly reopened the throttle, the train again started to gain speed. One of the three men stumbled and fell back, disappearing into the blackness. The two others continued on and climbed on the pilot of the engine. After a short distance, one lost his grip, fell off, and rolled into the flames along the track, while the other hung on for dear life.

Root, alone in the suffocating heat of the cab, suddenly felt dizzy, slumped over, and fainted. His hand left the open throttle as he rolled out of his seat onto the grating. No. 4 continued to reverse very slowly, but no one manned the controls.

The fire storm struck the cars, breaking the windows and sending tongues of fire into the coaches. Frightened passengers pulled down the rubber blinds, which in a moment burned away. Males soaked handkerchiefs and linen seat covers with water from the coolers, passing them to women and children. Standing at his post in his burning chair car wetting towels, porter John Blair remained oblivious to the flames swirling around him and gave no concern for his own life. He only thought about doing what he considered his duty. "John," he said to himself, "if there ever was a time you need to be cool and clear-headed it is right now."[11]

A more desperate and horrible situation could hardly be imagined. Women passed out and men screamed. The flames stripped the people on the vestibules and the car steps off the train, burning them to death along the right-of-way. William Blades was in the lavatory wetting towels with half a dozen other men. One turned to him and asked, "What chances do you think we have of getting out of this?" Blades shouted back, "About one in twenty thousand!" With that, the man started toward the back door and had to be forcibly restrained from jumping into the fire. In the first-class coach, State Senator Frank Daugherty's son, Otto, moaned, "Have we got to die, Papa, have we got to die?" Daugherty had hardly finished reassuring the youth when a large man with bulging eyes ran through the car screaming at the top of his lungs, "We are all going to heaven together!" What a time to express such sentiments, Daugherty thought. As the train bounced and lurched back up the track, heaven seemed a very real possibility to most of those on board. R. L. Gorman said, "It was as if one had been thrown through a white-hot, roaring furnace."[12]

Country people who lived near the railroad line saw the train as their only salvation. Passenger W. W. Cracy, a St. Paul physician, later told reporters, "Nearer and nearer the flames were approaching, and finally the engineer was compelled to reverse . . . leaving behind scores of unfortunate ones who had not been able to reach the train, their only available means of escape. Those on board could see many of them sink to the ground, exhausted and overcome by the terrible heat, never again to rise. Many came running across the fields from small settlements, hoping to escape on the train, but only disappointment and death awaited them. On rushed the train through the fiery, hot breath of the pursuing flames, for a stop would have been fatal to all on board."[13]

Conductor Sullivan believed that the train had gone less than a quarter of a mile before a mighty wave of fire struck at what he estimated to be more than sixty miles an hour. As he watched, all the windows broke on the west side of the combination car. Across the aisle, a man kicked out the glass and leaped through the window into the roaring inferno. Another man tried to follow, but Sullivan lunged and managed to pull him back, the erstwhile jumper severely cutting his wrist on the jagged glass. He asked Sullivan, "Can you do anything for my hand?" The conductor said no and ran back to the crowded first-class car, where there was a great deal of confusion and screaming. "With all my might I shouted to the people to keep quiet," he remembered, "as everything was going to be all right, and as soon as I succeeded in making myself understood it seemed to restore them to splendid order." Going on into one of the chair cars, he observed porter Blair administering to the wants of the passengers. Blair stood out as a tower of strength in the middle of the chaos and suffering, Sullivan calling him "as brave a man as I ever saw."[14]

As the train slowed perceptibly at the bottom of Hinckley Little Hill, Root opened his eyes, gradually regained his senses, and contemplated his surroundings. The train had gone between one and two miles with no one at the controls. From his position on the floor, Root peered up at the dials and what he saw shocked him — he had only "95 of steam," a dangerously low figure. Engine 69 was about to stop of its own accord. Root presumed that he had shut the steam off "to a certain extent"

when he fell over. Struggling to his feet, he mounted the driver's seat, turned the necessary dials, and opened the throttle. It was very dark, but he did not think that the train had as yet reached Skunk Lake.

Apparently, the tornado of fire had swept past the train and lifted off the ground, never to return to earth. Although the train burned from one end to another, the atmosphere seemed cooler, possibly why Root revived. Fireman McGowan, who noticed the change, climbed out of the tank, and by the time he returned to the cab, Root's head was swaying back and forth. He was again on the verge of collapse. As McGowan grabbed Root's shoulders to keep the engineer from falling off the seat, water from the fireman's coat sleeve splattered the engineer's face. Root said, "My God! Give me some more of that. Go and draw a pail of water." McGowan followed orders and Root dipped his hands into the pail. Looking at his puffed hands, he moaned, "My hands are all burnt. I don't dare rub them for fear of rubbing the flesh off." McGowan replied, "Mine are burnt, too," and thrust his hands into the water. Root took the pail and said, "Let me have it and put some more water in." When McGowan indicated that the tanks had hardly any left, Root, feeling "ninety per cent better immediately,"[15] told him instead to throw on more coal, which he did.

Noticing water in a ditch alongside the roadbed, Root realized within seconds that he had reached Skunk Lake. The next fifteen miles up the line held no more water and No. 69's tender was about to run dry. Applying the brakes, Root brought the train to a stop, only to realize that he had halted directly in the middle of a long and low bridge. With exasperation, he threw the reverse lever into forward motion, moved ahead a couple of lengths, and stopped again. He then fell prone onto the floor of the engine. The St. Paul & Duluth Railroad No. 4 limited of 1 September 1894 had made its last stop.

☆   ☆   ☆

The train had arrived at Skunk Lake sometime between 4:30 and 4:45 p.m. — accounts varied, the situation hardly conducive to official and bureaucratic calculations. The exact time of the run also differed: some people thought the trip lasted no more than five minutes, others thought at least twenty. Flames licking through windows, black swirling smoke, and waves of heat made it difficult to keep telling time. A few of those in the coaches estimated the running speed at a minimum of twenty-five miles per hour; others thought it much slower. Even the train crew had their doubts. With Root passed out and McGowan cowered in the tank, the rest of the men were too busy to notice. Of course, few on board expected to survive. Blades said in retrospect, "As for myself, I seemed to appreciate fully the fearfulness of the danger and the hopelessness of the situation, for I had given up the idea of ever getting out alive, and yet I must have been in a sort of daze, for the nearness of an extremely shocking death did not disturb me as much as it might have done, and I presume it very much the same with those around me."

Skunk Lake, about seven miles north of Hinckley, actually qualified as a slough, an uninviting sixty-acre stretch of dirty water about eighteen inches deep and located on the west side of the tracks in the middle of a two-hundred-acre meadow. Blades recalled, "When the train stopped and some said, 'This is the place!' it seemed natural enough that we should stop here, but it was not coupled with exquisite sense of relief, which is supposed to be experienced by those who have escaped a very great danger."[16]

Just after the train halted, Root felt weak and rolled off the seat to the floor. He told McGowan, "Leave me alone and go help the passengers into the water." McGowan retorted, "You can't live here."[17] Replying that he could take care of himself, Root again ordered the fireman to leave. McGowan finally left, then returned shortly with another man, and the two of them helped Root down from the cab and assisted him into the water, where a gradual numbness came over the lower half of his body.

All the coaches were in flames. Jumping to the ground, conductor Sullivan dashed through the fire. The first person he saw was fireman McGowan carrying an empty pail. Taking the pail away from him, Sullivan filled it with Skunk Lake water, which he threw on the coach platforms. Such a small amount of water seemed a futile gesture under the

58

circumstances. Porter Blair, taking more positive action, started directing passengers through an opening in a wire fence into Skunk Lake. One distraught man asked him why he had not put the fire out.[18]

Other persons found their way off the stricken train as best they could. James E. Lobdell, a traveling agent for Noyes Bros. & Cutler of St. Paul, described it as a scene from Dante's *Inferno*. He stated: "Men, women and children piled into the water in one heterogeneous mass. Everybody abandoned his baggage nor thought of aught else but saving his own life. I had a small traveling grip with me and carried it into the water. We had been in the water scarcely half a minute when through the wall of smoke there burst a sea of livid flame, crackling and roaring like a thousand demons in search of their prey. The heat was awful. Somebody shouted: 'Get under the water for your lives!' I obeyed the command, and I guess everybody else did likewise. I felt as though I was burning up. My mouth got dry and I could feel my tongue swelling. My eyeballs seemed starting out of my head, and for a moment I felt the flames above and seemingly all around me. I think I lost consciousness. I don't know how long I had myself completely submerged under the water. I suppose it was only a few minutes, but it seemed an age. When I raised my head the flames were roaring on at the south shore of the lake, having swept completely across the shallow body of water to the other side. All around the lake the woods were on fire, and a wall of flame seemingly 15 to 20 feet high completely hemmed us in. It was an awful, awe-inspiring sight, which I hope to never witness again. While I was watching the work of the flames all around, a red, lurid glare shot higher and brighter than the surrounding flame, and dimly through the smoke and flying sparks I could see that the train was all ablaze. The heat from the burning cars became so intense that once more we were compelled to seek relief under the water, raising our heads at brief intervals to get a breath of air so impregnated with smoke and fire that it was like poison to breathe it, and afforded us but little relief."[19]

Others had just as terrifying experiences. "A few of us were unable to reach the lake on account of the blinding smoke and intense heat," George Dunlap said. "We ran up the track and came to a culvert; into this wooden box we crawled, foolishly thinking that in it we might escape the scorching wind. In a short time we were driven out, but returned again and again, staying long enough to get fresh air. At last we were forced to leave the culvert and seek safety elsewhere. After roaming about aimlessly, we sat down in a place where there was nothing inflammable. There we remained with our heads covered with coats, while the storm of fire brands, cinders and ashes swept over us. Thus we escaped suffocation. Our eyes filled with dust and weakened by heat, began to cause us intense suffering."[20]

After watching some of the male passengers kick the staples off the barbed-wire fence that separated the roadbed from the lake, William Blades ran through the gap and on into the marsh. "'Here I sat down with the rest so that the mire and water came up nearly to the armpits," he recalled, "and when sheets of flame swept over us, as they seemed to do periodically, we would crouch down as much as possible, keeping our heads entirely covered with wet clothing."[21]

Senator Daugherty and his son Otto, upon discovering themselves virtually alone on the burning train, climbed off, found some tall grass, and lay down. They had no way of knowing in the darkness that they were on the edge of a slough. After a short time, they moved to higher ground. Two sisters, Annie Kernan and Mrs. Minnie Spriggs, had arrived there ahead of them, the latter cradling a little baby in her arms. When sheets of flame rocketed through the patch, Daugherty threw his body over his son, but the women screamed as their heavy and cumbersome clothing caught fire. "Don't let the poor lady burn up, papa, I am all right," Otto cried.[22] Responding at once, the senator succeeded in tearing away the burning parts of the dresses. As sheets of fire continued to roar across the potato patch, he had to repeat the process two more times.

All was confusion and horror. Believing it safer to stay on the train, two Chinamen refused to leave their seats and burned to death within minutes. Another passenger ran north down the track, vanishing into a mass of flames, never again seen alive. Mrs. Lawrence, carrying a babe in arms, went south, finally falling down between the rails. She fought desperately to put out the flames that licked at her dress, to no avail. Mrs. John McNamara and two of her sons, all of whom had escaped from Hinckley on the train, ran north up the tracks until the flames caught them and burned them beyond recognition. Another son, Peter McNamara, successfully sought safety in the muck of Skunk Lake.[23] The man who had clung to the pilot survived the trip and ran into the marsh. C. A. Vandever heard a woman scream, "Help me! Help me! I am burning!" After beating out the flames in her hair with his bare hands, he led her into the lake.[24] Molly McNeil, a refugee from Hinckley, jumped off the bridge, rolled in the mud to put out the fire in her clothes, found shelter behind an old barrel, and discovered a large snake coiled beside her. She dared not move.[25] Some people who had rushed to the platforms jumped off while the train was still moving. Others fought their way through the struggling mass of passengers. Many persons suffered severe injuries, including broken bones and limbs.

C. D. O'Brien had no sooner left his coach than he heard someone yell that people should get back inside. A few women tried and needed restraining. O'Brien and about two other persons crawled toward the fence, which seemed about fifty feet away. Although the heat was suffocating and cinders pelted down out of the smoke cover, the group made it through the fence and twenty feet farther on reached sandy soil. "There again the sirocco-like hot air almost overwhelmed us, but we lay prone upon the ground, and by keeping our faces almost buried in the sand succeeded in escaping suffocation," O'Brien recounted.[26] One of the young men in the group reported seeing water to the south, that he had caught the glint of it as the train stopped. Moreover, they thought they saw John Blair standing to the south, sprinkling water from an extinguisher on prostrate women and children. They returned and easily persuaded the rest to follow. Although they could not see objects at a distance of more than a few feet, they all reached the water. Within a short time, O'Brien concluded that the full weight of the fire had passed over and that they were standing in the center of a meadow. He was able to see by the light of the burning coaches.

Conductor Sullivan realized that someone had to inform the outside world what had happened to No. 4. Approximately 300 people lay prostrate in the vicinity of Skunk Lake. After the last great rushes of hot air had rolled across the stricken company, he decided to go two miles farther up the line to Miller, the next station. Technically, he abandoned people under his responsibility, but extenuating circumstances demanded it. Porter Blair had the situation under control in the marsh where he had taken unequivocal and unchallenged command. Time and again he had returned to the cars, directing shocked people to safety. In the lake he personified strength, giving orders and standing amidst the flames with a fire extinguisher, from which he sprayed water onto burning clothing. For the moment, no one concerned himself with Blair's race. So, Sullivan felt free to leave.[27]

Gritting his teeth and shielding his face as best he could, the conductor started up the track. When a woman asked Sullivan where he was going, he replied, "For help," and disappeared up the line into the smoke. He later composed a carefully worded statement in which he explained: "When I thought everything else was secure I then thought of getting some report to my superior officers, so as to get some assistance for those suffering people. I started on my perilous walk through smoke and heat. The smoke was so dense that I could not see my open hand before me. I kept, all this time, between the rails of the track, lest I should wander away from it and be burned. I had to lie down at various times on the ground in order to get a breath of air, and suffered intense pain with my eyes." At Miller Station, Sullivan found telegrapher Thompson at his post. Sullivan learned that local freight No. 12 was at the Willow River and that the bridges were still open above Miller. Before the heat made it necessary to abandon the station, Thompson sent to Duluth "a portion of a message" Sullivan had composed. The two men, along with Thompson's wife and two children, left three minutes before it burned to the ground. They then trudged up the line toward Finlayson Station, four miles away.[28]

Back at Skunk Lake the survivors cowered in the marsh. The Red Demon, advancing in the wake of the tornado, roared through in a terrible billow of fire. L. S. Meeker tried to convey the horror of the situation to a journalist: "I wish I were able to describe the scene as it appeared from our place of safety at Skunk Lake. But that no man on earth can do. Great clouds of smoke rolled above us, carrying burning embers a great length. The trees on all sides of us were ablaze, and being of varying heights the scene presented was that of a lighted city upon a dark night. The roar of the wind was something terrible to hear. It was impossible to hear each other speak, and the only human sound was an occasional scream of some one struck by a flying ember or otherwise injured. The fire was in a few minutes of passing out of sight, leaving only dead trees and the leaves and smaller branches of green ones burning."[29] The remains of the limited smouldered on the track while frightened people prayed and hoped that help was coming.

Chapter 4

"Make for the River"

As the St. Paul & Duluth limited train slowed to a stop at Skunk Lake, combination train No. 24 was somewhere on the nine miles of Eastern Minnesota track between Hinckley and Sandstone. The passengers and refugees, jammed in the caboose, three boxcars, and five coaches, could see nothing except smoke and flickers of flame. Although they could hear a roaring sound, they had no way of knowing it was a tornado of fire less than four miles away, passing them and rolling toward the north. Even if they had been aware of what was happening on the other track, they probably would not have cared except in an abstract sense. The horrors of the destruction of Hinckley remained fresh in their minds and they had their own troubles to worry about.

The train crew worried about the bridges. On the tender of freight engineer Edward Barry's Engine No. 105, four brakemen, C. Beach from passenger No. 4, plus G. Gilliam, P. McLaughlin, and C. C. Freeman of the freight, peered and squinted down the line, trying to identify objects. They doused themselves with water from the tank as they stayed at their dangerous posts. Freeman had the responsibility of signaling Barry when to throttle or brake. Barry then had to whistle the instructions back to passenger engineer William Best, bringing up the rear in Engine No. 125. It was at best a complicated and unwieldy arrangement.

As the train approached a forty-foot-high trestle, which burned in several places, Freeman briefly considered stopping and called for brakes. Back in No. 125, Best, who had been apprehensive about crossing the structure, felt his heart "chilled" by the whistle. Turning to fireman George Ford, he moaned, "George, the jig is up. The train is lost and all that are on board

64

of it." No reply came. Both men remained tense, Best thinking of the censure he would face for holding the train too long in Hinckley. "The fear of death never entered my mind," he recalled. "There was no room for any other sensation than remorse and self-condemnation for what I then believed to have been my bad judgment."[1] He thought he suffered more than at any other time in his life. Then, just as he had given up, Barry, following Freeman's orders, signaled the go ahead. Best, "gladdened" by the shrill sound, released the brakes and opened the throttle. The train rolled on through the smoke, crossing one burning bridge after another.

Watching from the moving train, Judge Seagrave Smith had seen a tongue of flame incinerate a woman and two children who were fleeing towards the gravel pit. That was his last memory of Hinckley, but he had no time to dwell on the ghastly event. He concentrated instead on his own fate. He saw what he believed to be walls of fire for long distances along the roadway. "Nothing in my opinion prevented our car from taking fire, excepting that the right of way on each side was very well cleared of combustible matter and the wind was blowing directly in the line of the track," he declared. "Had it been blowing across the track nothing could have saved us. All must have perished."[2]

No. 24 backed into Sandstone and came to a stop. The usual quota of station house loungers stood around. The wild-eyed occupants of the freight and passenger cars exhorted and pleaded with the people on the platform to climb aboard and escape for their lives; Hinckley had gone and Sandstone would go next. Only a few got on board. Those at the station ignored all the signs — the reversed combination train full of fleeing refugees, the steadily rising wind, the gradually increasing heat, and the thick black smoke billowing all around. For reasons known only to themselves, most decided that they would stay and make a stand in Sandstone.[3]

The conductors and engineers held a hasty meeting on the platform to decide what to do next. Both conductors, William

Campbell of the freight and H. D. Powers of the passenger,
wanted to remain in Sandstone. No one had any way of knowing about conditions up the track; the bridges might have burned
down or the rails could have warped. Barry and Best talked
it over, both wanting to leave as soon as possible. After a few
minutes, Barry, the chief engineer by virtue of his authority
over No. 24 — under railroad regulations No. 4 no longer existed
— spoke for himself and his older and more experienced col-
league. He explained that he was not going to stay, because
remaining meant sure death. Sandstone was going to burn.
Looking at him, Powers said in a matter-of-fact voice, "All right,
go ahead. You are running the engine and have the right of the
road." Best added, "We want to get out as quickly as possible,
for the fire is coming on us fast!"[4] They had made a hard decision in the gloom of the Sandstone Station. As the railroaders
climbed back on the train, they knew what lay ahead — the
Kettle River bridge.

The long and high Kettle River bridge stood two miles north
of Sandstone. One of the two watchmen on the great wooden
structure, M. W. W. Jesmer, had grown apprehensive about
4:00 p.m., as a fire started in the woods on the left side of the
tracks. When the wind rose and sparks pelted down on the
bridge, Jesmer ran to his nearby house and told his little boy
to go into Sandstone to tell the section foreman to dispatch a
crew of firemen as a precautionary measure. Shortly, Peter
Peterson, the station agent and quarry superintendent in Sandstone, appeared, shouting that the southbound passenger had
reversed and would pass over the bridge in a few minutes.
Jesmer told his wife to go down to the river and hurried back
toward the trestle where, to his horror, he saw that the structure was on fire in "twenty or thirty places" and that the sparks
falling "thick and fast" looked like hailstones. Jesmer had not
reached the bridge when the train arrived. However, W. W.
Damuth, the elderly night watchman, had stayed at his duty
post.[5]
     While Barry slowed to the required four miles an hour and
watched for the company signals to cross the structure, Best
waited apprehensively in the rear locomotive. Damuth, yell-
ing, "For God's sake, go on, you can cross it now and it will

go down in five minutes,"[6] waved No. 24 over the bridge. Barry and Best breathed collective sighs of relief as the heavy train clacked over the bridge and picked up speed on the other side. It seemed routine to the crew members.

Jesmer saw the whole panorama. "The train had not gone more than two thousand feet from the bridge when the two beams on the east side were blown over," he declared. "I knew then that the bridge was doomed, and so went back to my house to try to save what I could."[7] After carrying a heavy trunk full of belongings to a nearby potato field, he started down the bluff to find his wife. On the way he observed Damuth standing some distance from the bridge, apparently in a daze. He failed to answer a call from Jesmer to run for the river, and subsequently perished in the fire.

Because the train was running ahead of the flames, it chugged the next seven miles to the small lumber camp of Partridge without further incident. Although the smoke remained thick, none of the bridges were on fire. The station was a welcome sight to the train crew for both engines needed water and coal. During the watering operations, passengers came up to the engines looking for drinking water. Many people had passed out from the heat and the cramped quarters. While engineer Barry and brakeman Freeman led a group of men to the O'Neil logging camp for pails and cups, the rest of the brakemen and the two conductors went through the train trying to do what they could to alleviate the suffering.

A railroad dispatch awaited engineer Barry and freight No. 24 in Partridge. Sent earlier in the day, it noted certain routing changes between Partridge and the yards in West Superior. The new orders informed Barry that he had a clear track the rest of the way. Extra freight No. 22 from West Superior to St. Cloud had been stopped at Dedham, Wisconsin, about fifteen miles south of Duluth-Superior. The afternoon No. 3 passenger from Minneapolis would run late and follow No. 24 up the line. The telegram concluded by stating that Barry should use his own judgment. The tired engineer read the contents without comment. He had not thought about the possibility of No. 3 running down his train — obviously, it could not get past Hinckley. Nor had he expected a freight to come thundering down the line. As for the last part of the message, he felt he had been using his own judgment since reaching Hinckley earlier in the afternoon. After putting the piece of paper in his pocket, he climbed back into his cab, whistled his intentions to start, and opened his throttle.[8]

No. 24 backed out of Partridge toward safety, having stopped an estimated twenty to twenty-five minutes. The residents of Partridge stood in small groups watching it go up the line. After they heard the last whistles in the distance, they turned away from the railroad and contemplated how to defend their settlement, if the fire arrived. As in Sandstone, no one got on the train, even though thick and sooty billows of smoke rolled over the settlement, and the smell of tar permeated the air. One citizen who saw the train wrote: "It stopped briefly and we were urged to get on board but, strangely, we all refused like one man, for what reason I still fail to understand, and the train left."[9]

The conflagration that destroyed Hinckley had sent heat, fire bolts, and even a blazing tornado ahead. Now, its forces consolidated, it began a calculated advance toward Sandstone. It left behind distressed land, dismembered bodies, and dazed survivors. Ahead lay new territories to conquer and victims to kill. The Red Demon continued to stalk the great pine forests of Minnesota.

Mrs. Garrity was the madam at a house of prostitution located in the woods north of Hinckley on the government road. Until late in the afternoon she primarily had concerned herself with preparations for the evening business activities. This changed after 4:00 p.m., when she realized that a monstrous fire was sweeping toward her establishment. She grabbed a roll of bills, tucked them into a black lace stocking, and yelled, "Get going, girls." The four inmates, clad in red shirtwaists and petticoats, hustled after her down a long path that led to a pool by the Grindstone River. All made the cooling waters with no trouble, except for "Big Mary," a five-foot-tall girl of three hundred pounds, who waddled along behind. Although hot cinders set her hair and clothes on fire, she continued doggedly onward, while behind her the house burst into flames. She staggered along, eventually falling into the water like a great whale, where she huddled with her colleagues.[10]

A half mile south of Sandstone a young farm couple, Alfred Broad and his wife, decided to stay at their small house. A son and daughter instinctively trusted their parents' judgment. After fire was all around, the family made a run toward the north, heading in the general direction of the Kettle River. The little girl died first. Next, the flames struck down the mother and after that the father. The nine-year-old son went a little farther before the fire closed around him.

Another farmer, Lars Mattis, intended to battle the holocaust. Soon giving up, he descended a ladder into a deep well, taking a bundle of clothing along with him. As the well had several feet of water at the bottom, Mattis initially considered himself safe. Sparks, however, showered down the shaft, igniting the bundle. A wave of heat followed. He felt sick and on the verge of passing out.[11]

Peter Peterson, the quarry superintendent and station agent in Sandstone, had spent an uneasy day. After the sky darkened around 2:00 p.m., he sent his crew home from the pit. When he went to his store, the darkness necessitated his lighting the lamps, and he saw men carrying lanterns in the streets. Shortly after No. 4 passed south around 3:00 p.m., a small fire started about 600 feet from the station. After ordering the quarry's second shift to take the horses out of the company barn and to assemble barrels of water, Peterson went home, convinced that he had taken correct precautionary measures. A short while later bridge watchman M. W. W. Jesmer's son knocked on the door and told him about the danger to the Kettle River bridge. Peterson hurried to the structure, arriving shortly before No. 24 backed across. After the train went over — he did not think the bridge on fire — Peterson walked back toward town.

He soon had to make a decision about what to do next. Later, he recalled: "Just then, I heard a rumbling noise which I thought was thunder. I could see the fire in the sky across the river; it looked as though a cyclone were coming upon us, carrying everything before it, then it died down and I thought the danger had passed. Shortly after that, a strong wind came up from the southwest; I then realized that there would be no chance of saving the town." He may or may not have seen the fire storm that engulfed the St. Paul & Duluth train. The gigantic forest fire unleashed several tornados of fire.

Running to his store, Peterson told his wife and children to go outside. Before he left, he carefully extinguished the lamps and locked the door, then, standing in front, he pondered what to do. A man raced past, shouting, "Make for the river!" Given the roar of the fire, it took Peterson several seconds to comprehend what he had heard. Eventually, he decided to go to the Kettle River, about 800 yards away. "When we were on the main road which led to it, the people of the town were coming from all directions, and before we got half way down to the river, the brush, trees, and houses on both sides of the road were burning," he said. "I thought we could find sufficient protection behind a pile of small stones on the river bank, but the heat was so intense that we did not stay there longer than three or four minutes. We all went into the river, which is, at this place, about two feet deep."[12] Since the wind and heat made it impossible to stand in the water, the people started throwing water over each other.

The Lifebrer residence stood in the middle of a Sandstone clearing, approximately 200 yards from the nearest trees. David Lifebrer, who was in Dakota following the harvest, had many mouths to feed. On the afternoon of 1 September, two of his seven children were doing chores around Sandstone, while the rest, including a five-month-old baby, were at home with their mother. She busied herself entertaining two visitors, her brother-in-law, Peter Bilado, and one of his daughters, both of whom lived on a farm northeast of Sandstone.

When the sky grew darker and darker, Mrs. Lifebrer lighted the kerosene lamps at 4:00 p.m. Fire reflected in the sky, and the woods on one side of the clearing burst into flames. About 5:30 p.m., balls of fire shot overhead. Loud retorts made sounds like falling timber, the wind rose, and sparks flew in all directions. Despite these unsettling developments, Mrs. Lifebrer remained confident right up to the last minute. "I thought we were safe, as our house stands in the middle of a clearing," she averred.

With startling fury, the dwelling burst into flames. Mrs. Lifebrer, carrying the baby in a shawl, ran toward plowed ground about twenty yards away, her other children, ages three to sixteen, following. The family group buried themselves as best they could in the loose dirt. The air seemed full of hot sand as they tried to ward the particles off by covering themselves with a heavy shawl. Their cat ran out of the woods and crawled under.

Peter Bilado and his daughter had hurried to a drainage ditch, about fifty yards from the house. When the long grass on either side started to burn and set their clothing ablaze, Bilado beat at the flames with his bare hands. The girl, overcome with fear, jumped to her feet and dashed directly into the fire, calling out, "Papa, Papa!" Bilado, too stunned to act, remained in the ditch. Nearly all his clothes burned off his body and cinders pelted down like hail.

Mrs. Lifebrer's other two children fared as best they could. Her eldest son, driving home when the fire struck, cut the team loose and sought safety in a corn field. The younger boy, who was at the post office, wanted to go home, but people would not let him. Eventually, he went with them to the river bank.[13]

When Superintendent Peterson terminated the first shift at the quarry, one worker, Patrick Regan, had quickly walked the half mile to his house. When he arrived, it became necessary to put on the lamps. The darkness caused him to ask a neighbor what was the matter. When the neighbor asserted it was an eclipse of the sun and that the sky would clear shortly, Regan found that difficult to believe. He said it had to be either a fire or a cyclone. As they argued, the sky turned bright red, convincing both it was a fire. Regan rushed back into his home and ordered his family to go to the river while he remained and poured water onto two stacks of hay in the backyard.

After three houses in the vicinity caught fire and large balls of flame hurtled out of the smoke cover, he decided that the whole business was absolutely hopeless. As he started toward the river, he remembered his cow. Running back, he cut her loose in the burning barn, got her out the door, and headed her in the general direction of the river, following as fast as he could. He saw a woman come running from another direction. As he watched, the flames overtook her and she slowed and dropped to the ground. Regan turned and dashed on. By the time he reached the water and plunged in, his clothing had caught fire.

Regan looked up at the bank and saw about fifty persons who appeared afraid to go into the water. After he pulled four into the water, the rest gradually followed on their own. He then discovered that two of his children were missing. Separated from the main body, they crouched on the bank, too frightened to move. Regan carried one into the river, where she clung to him with all her might. When he saw his faithful dog Prince, he told him to go rescue the other daughter, Lizzie. Prince was up to the challenge. He bounded up the bank, ran to Lizzie, and dragged her into the water. After that they could do nothing except wait for the fire to pass.[14]

The Reverend Emil Anderson, the young and handsome pastor of the Swedish Congregational Church in Sandstone, planned to leave shortly for the Chicago Theological Seminary and his last year in divinity school. On Friday evening, 31 August, he had delivered a farewell sermon in Hinckley. After briefly considering staying overnight, he had caught the 3:00 a.m. northbound St. Paul & Duluth milk train. Although fires on either side of the line stopped the train from time to time, this had not bothered Pastor Anderson: forest fires had been burning all summer around Hinckley and Sandstone. Getting off at Miller at 4:00 a.m., he walked the four miles to Sandstone, arriving at first light and with a guilty conscience. His flock in the predominantly Swedish community had planned an "entertainment" for him the coming evening, and he had yet to compose a sermon. When he reached his rooms, he went right to work instead of going to bed. Words failed to come and in early afternoon he still struggled, trying to find something appropriate to say. As he stared out the window, he lost his train of thought with a start. The sky had turned red; Anderson thought it looked as if it were "dipped in blood."

Going into the streets, he did what he could to help prepare

72

for a possible conflagration. As volunteers pulled out the fire apparatus, the pump operator at the waterworks increased pressure. After Anderson saw a telegraph message from Hinckley, which stated, "If you love your lives, try to save them," he hurried around town telling everyone he saw to go to the river. Some did, some did not. The man at the waterworks refused to leave his post, convinced that if he did his superintendent would fire him. Another person planned to use six barrels and four washtubs full of water to protect himself, his family, and his home. The loungers at the station laughed at the possible danger. Three families started toward the river, a woman with a babe in arms lagging behind. Suddenly, a wind gust picked her up, carried her thirty feet through the air into a corn field, then threw her to the ground. Anderson ran into the field where he found her standing unharmed, holding her child. After taking the baby, he told the woman to follow him to the water. The wind picked him up, and he sailed an estimated 1,000 feet before being gently dropped to earth. He landed on his feet still holding the child, only a couple of feet from the river. A short distance away the mother, carried along for the second time, stood unharmed. Jumping in the water, Anderson and the woman became separated, but he found her husband and gave him the child. Men, women, and children who had been standing on the west bank plunged into the stream. Above, the fire soared "sky high." In the distance, Anderson heard the "awful cries and wailings" from the townspeople who had ignored the warnings to flee for their lives.[15] Few who had not heeded the first warnings to flee to the river survived. The aged H. S. Hoffman and his wife expired within fifty feet of their house. Edward Johnson died just beyond the door of his store. Peter Englund and others jumped in a well; it was dry, had a wooden top, boarded walls, and burned like a torch. Although Mrs. Gustaf Anderson and her children fled their dwelling, she died in a well, the children on the run.[16] The flames flared all around.

The Friesendahls, who lived on the outskirts of Sandstone, did not comprehend the danger until black clouds darkened the sun and the air seemed on the verge of igniting into flames. Nine-year-old Axel Friesendahl recalled, "Mother said for us kids to beat it for the river. They gathered up what they could carry and came behind us." Running down an old quarry trail, the family plunged into the water just before the full force of the fire arrived. Axel saw forms surging overhead, "going about 100 miles an hour." He thought they were ordinary clouds until one crashed into the bluff on the other side of the Kettle River, setting fire to the entire hillside. Another cloud of hot gas struck the trestle. "It was like someone pressed a lever and it all caught fire," he said. "The wind started the whole thing at once."[17]

On the family's isolated farm northeast of Sandstone, Mrs. Peter Bilado knew that a big fire burned near Hinckley, but she had not given it much thought. On the late afternoon of 1 September, she was sitting on her doorstep cradling her baby, waiting for the other children to bring the cows in from the pasture. By 5:00 p.m. they had driven the cows into the barn and fifteen minutes later Mrs. Bilado and her children sat down for supper. Shortly after 5:30 p.m., when they saw the woods burning about a quarter of a mile away, Mrs. Bilado let the stock loose, for a while thinking she could save the house with a couple of buckets of water. When this became impractical, she and her children started toward McKay's Lake. Holding the baby with one arm, she carried a pail of water on the other. Fourteen-year-old Flora lugged a sheet and two blankets, the remaining two girls clutching their mother's dress. They had progressed no more than fifty yards when flames overtook them, burning cinders falling like flakes of snow. Mrs. Bilado threw water on the sheet and told the children to lie under it in the rutabaga patch. Then, for inexplicable reasons, she started back to the pump to draw more water. After filling the pail, she began the return trip. First, a falling limb knocked the pail out of her hand and spilled most of the water. Second, a deer bounded up to her as if seeking protection. Appearing dazed, the animal jumped off a short distance and dropped dead in its tracks. By the time Mrs. Bilado reached her children the wind howled with cyclonic force, pushing hot air through the field.

When Flora asked if they were all going to die, her mother replied that they should trust God to do what was right for all of them. She tried to spread the wet sheet over her children, but the wind carried it away. The flames roared, making a noise like thunder. When Flora suddenly stood up, saying she was going to look for the sheet that had blown away, her mother told her not to go. She either did not hear, did not understand, did not know what she was doing, or had made up her mind. After running about 100 yards directly toward the fire, Flora vanished in the flames. Mrs. Bilado screamed, although she could do nothing. She put out fires in her hair and dress by tossing dirt on the burning places. When the baby gagged, she blew in his mouth and revived him. The two other children lay still in the dirt. Until they stirred, Mrs. Bilado had no way of knowing whether they were dead or alive. Then, as suddenly as it had arrived, the fire swept past and on to the north. Mrs. Bilado rose and looked around. She recalled, "Nothing was to be seen: fire everywhere. I thought of my poor Flora and wondered if she had suffered much."[18]

Near Finlayson, Thomas J. Henderson of Pine City and his fourteen- and sixteen-year-old sons were building a new logging road for the St. Paul & Duluth Railroad. They were working hard when, without warning, the fire bore down upon them. After it ended, the grim-faced father talked about what happened: "We had noticed things looked a little threatening, but anticipated no danger until the fire was nearly upon us when we started for Mr. Greenfield's home about a quarter of a mile east of the track. When we reached there we found the family going to the cellar of the house and we went in with them. We had been there but a short time when it became apparent that none of us would escape if we staid there long, so we crawled out and ran for a potato patch close by. Our clothes were burning as we left the cellar, and I had a hard fight to put out the blaze. After I did so, the boys one after the other became overcome with the heat and died right before my eyes."

M. E. Greenfield, a Swede who had changed his name from Grönfält, his wife, their four girls and two sons, plus the hired hand, John Parrish, had gone to the cellar expecting a cyclone. When the dining room table crashed through the floor, they all ran to the field. The heat was terrible and the fiery wind tore great trees up by the roots. Finding an ox, Parrish grabbed its tail, and disappeared into the blazing woods. Greenfield's fifteen-year-old girl ran back into the burning house, where flames consumed her. Three other daughters, ages three, five, and eight, plus a seven-year-old son, lost consciousness and died. Before passing out, farmer Greenfield had torn the flaming clothing off his daughters' backs. His ten-year-old son, Charlie, who had rolled in the dirt to avoid burning to death, roused him. Together, they aroused Mrs. Greenfield. The air cleared and the worst appeared over, although the dead remained, still on the ground.[19]

The wind usually drops in early evening; that of the great fire was no exception. When the fire reached Partridge in early twilight, fifty residents, all from five families, had time to escape, although the "mighty wall of smoke" arrived sooner than expected. Putting the women and children on railroad hand-cars, the men took them three miles up the Eastern Minnesota line to a 100-acre tract of burned-over country. Some men walked; only one, Robert Burns, did not make it. He burned to death along the tracks. "All the time the fire was right behind us," a member of the party explained. "The smoke had gathered again and thickened into a grayish black mass which rolled forward at an incredible speed with a deafening roar, whining and rumbling. We had barely reached our place of refuge when the great wall of smoke behind us split, or rather, was flung asunder, and a blood-red flame of fire shot out like a flash of lightning. In a moment every particle of smoke had disappeared and in its place we saw a sea of fire as far as the eye could scan. A short time before a mighty green forest had stood there, proudly waving its crowns. To our inexpressible joy we saw that our place of refuge offered a safe harbor, as the fire billowed on both sides but was unable to reach or harm us and at the edge of the clearing to the south, the waves of fire fell powerless."[20] While the persons in the clearing had much to mourn, they had survived.

Sometime during the early evening hours the Red Demon halted and did not continue. He reached cutover at the Wisconsin border, the temperature inversion that spawned him no longer determining weather patterns in the Upper Midwest. Between midday and early evening the monster had ravaged some of the best remaining virgin timber on the North American continent. He cut a swath approximately thirty miles wide and thirty miles long through the wilderness, destroying over 900 square miles of territory. Pokegama, Mission Creek, Hinckley, Miller, Sandstone, and Partridge all burned to the ground. Over 2,000 persons lost their homes. Hundreds perished. Unfortunately, the last rush of flames did not end matters: the rescue efforts remained, as did the cold and analytical accounting of the magnitude of the tragedy.

The Reverend Anderson, standing in the Kettle River, thought that the fire brought the survivors closer to God. "In this, our great common despair, we were all praying people; Christians or non-Christians," he said. "The ungodly of all kinds prayed now to the living God, if they never had prayed before."[21] Someone found a great flat block of stone out in the river. After Anderson with about 100 people reached the rock, they gathered around him and held a prayer meeting. At the conclusion, they raised their voices and praised God with an English version of the Swedish hymn, "The Mighty Fortress," the first and last stanzas of which are:[22]

> To the rock that's higher, take me
> From the flames across Jordan's stream,
> Take me to that mighty fortress
> Which in every storm shall stand.
>
> Rock of Ages, give, oh give me,
> Strength to sing the praise of love;
> With the roaring flames around me,
> 'Till I rest in peace above.

Chapter 5

"The Country Is All Burning Up"

A thickening volume of smoke riding a fresh southwest wind rolled over Duluth-Superior. Falling ashes left a thick coating on the pavement. By 4:00 p.m., lights burned brightly along downtown streets, in office buildings, and other commercial establishments. "The smoke has been almost suffocating in Duluth this afternoon," the *Evening Herald* reported, "owing to a change in wind bringing smoke from extensive fires which are burning the country to the south and west."[1] It seemed fairly certain that something awful was happening in the pineries. When ill-concealed uneasiness in railroad circles added to a growing panic, businesses closed and people flocked into the streets. Few went home. Many stood in hushed groups, not knowing what to do or what was going to happen next. For the moment, Duluth-Superior appeared in little danger, but the affected areas were all part of the twin ports' immediate marketing hinterlands. In addition to important business connections, numerous persons had relatives, friends, and acquaintances in the burning forests. Crowding around the telegraph offices, a large number of anxious watchers waited for dispatches from Hinckley or other points to the south, while operators hunched over the silent keys, hoping for transmissions.

At 5:55 p.m., C. M. Phillips, a telegrapher at the general freight office of the St. Paul & Duluth Railroad, sat up with a start. A message was coming in, datelined Miller Station, 1 September. Clearly delayed, the communication had passed through several operators on its way to Duluth. It stated: "The country is all burning up, No. 4 is burned up. Send relief,"[2] ending abruptly without any indication of the sender's name. Phillips wasted no time on speculation about why the wire went silent. He immediately sent instructions to conductor John Roper, who waited at Kettle River with No. 12 way-freight. The urgent message ordered: "Take engine, caboose and box-cars and go to relief of No. 4 passenger, as Miller reports they are burned up. Hurry for God's sake."[3] Under routine railroad procedures, the wire went out over the name of Dave H. Williams, the St. Paul & Duluth yardmaster in Duluth. After quickly sending other messages, Phillips stopped all normal down traffic on the railroad and ordered the "Short Line" passenger, due in Duluth Depot at 6:15, held for emergency duty.

Yardmaster Williams hurried to the station platform, planning to turn the "Short Line" into a relief train. Railroad representatives informed physicians and others responsible for disaster relief. The first dreadful news from the south had a tonic effect in Duluth-Superior. While the full ramifications of the disaster remained unclear, it was now possible to do something. The hastily made-up relief train pulled out at 7:05 p.m., loaded with workers, medical supplies, and food. Williams, General Agent C. M. Vance, four physicians — Magie, Codding, McCormick, and Gilbert — and two members of the press were on board.[4]

Great whirlwinds of flames flashed in the early evening sky with a strange and awful result that left viewers with a depressed feeling. The sky did not light up from one direction, nor was there a single bright glow. The whole vault of heaven became a glowing furnace dull and ruddy in color, with the appearance of intense heat. The phenomenon, at least fifty miles to the south of Duluth-Superior, appeared outside the range of known denominators. The firmament seemed a vast mass of molten metal threatening universal destruction. Many Scandinavians thought it looked like Ragnarök — the end of the world in Norse mythology.[5] Of course, the observers had no way of knowing that the worst was over, that the great sweep of fire had run its course. It was devouring the remains inside the burned districts.

The terrible heat abated in the vicinity of Pokegama — the first settled territory struck by the Red Demon. After spending several hours standing in cramped quarters in the water at the bottom of their well, the Kelsey family started shivering as the fear of heat gave way to that of cold. Lucy talked things over with her husband, who had a severe arm cramp, and at length they decided they could safely venture back to the surface. One after another they emerged into a blackened, dreary waste that stretched as far as the eye could see. A shocked Lucy recorded what she saw: "Not a timber left of the house, only a gaping, smoking cellar. All the beautiful trees laid low, only the dark trunks left; all smoking, many still burning. Nothing green in all the world, and waves of scorching heat rising all about us as we stood bareheaded and soiled and panting by the ruins of our home." Near the well lay an axe and hammer, both virtually undamaged, having only blackened handles. Looking down into the cellar, the Kelseys identified parts of the sewing machine, remnants of the stove, and some broken dishes — the fire and heat had melted or consumed all their other belongings.

Mr. Kelsey decided that they must leave as soon as possible to find shelter. When his family asked if they could at least remain long enough to dry their clothes, he replied, "No, night is coming on. We must try and find a place of shelter." He and his oldest son, Allen, led the way, both lugging heavy, wet blankets, while Lucy carried little Lyle in her arms. Earl, who was barefoot, needed carrying over burning ground, and Maidie brought up the rear, complaining as always, "Oh, oh, I am burning my feet." The forlorn company, silhouetted against the darkening sky, stumbled along, hurrying over crisped grass and keeping away from burning stumps. Lucy had a severe headache. Her husband stopped to rest at intervals, frequently dropping to the ground and putting his hands over his eyes. When they finally reached Dr. C. A. Kelsey's potato patch, they looked in the direction of where his house had stood — there was nothing except ruins. "Oh, where can they be?" thought Lucy, with a sinking heart. It seemed improbable that any living thing had survived.

Walking on toward Pokegama, they crossed tangled telegraph wires, smoking ties, and hot rails. As they passed the burned ruins of the Nelson and Baty houses, they heard only the sound of a cowbell. Trudging on, they reached the bank above the pond near the railroad bridge and looked upon a welcome and, at the same time, unpleasant sight. Many friends and neighbors stood beside the water, according to Lucy in "attitudes betokening despair, suffering and hopeless misery." Almost instantly, they recognized Dr. Kelsey's wife and three children. "Oh, there they are!" exclaimed Maidie. Lucy, after being helped down the bank, said, "Oh, my dear sister, you do not know how relieved I feel to find you safe. But where is Doctor?" The distraught woman said that she thought her husband was dead. Two of the men with him when the fire struck, John Gonyea, who found shelter in a small pool, and Charles Collier, who reached the pond, both thought Dr. Kelsey perished.

The thirty or so survivors stood around the edge of the pond as if in a daze, many covering their smarting eyes with wet towels. Mrs. Carver and Mrs. Baty huddled together, sharing a quilt. One boy lay face down by his mother's side, while another sat with a hat concealing his face. Mrs. Berg, wrapped in a blanket, lay on the ground, surrounded by her little girls. John Gonyea contemplated his burned hands and feet. Mrs. Nelson and her two small children formed another pathetic group. Mrs. Seymour dropped to her knees, obviously suffering. Lucy recalled, "All were quiet and patient. No one groaned, none of the children cried, but the calm endurance all but added to the terrible pathos of the scene. Calling Maidie to hold my head, I stepped to one side and obtained relief to some extent from the racking headache I had been suffering since leaving the well. A second vomiting spell an hour or so later completed the cure."[6]

More refugees gradually appeared, including the two sisters who had huddled in a culvert. A small boy chanted over and over, "All yi, all yi." Someone dug potatoes for a possible supper; others tore up aprons for bandages. Men made a crude canopy out of water-soaked blankets. Mr. Ward remarked, "Friends, we are all on a level now." After making that statement, he walked off to look for shelter. When he returned about an hour later he reported that he had discovered two boxcars on a side track a mile down the Eastern Minnesota tracks. Miraculously, they had survived the fire. Although it was growing dark, many saw no particular advantage in leaving the pond. Thirteen, however, decided to go, including the Kelseys. They walked over the burning and smoking railroad ties to the cars. "While walking to the train, we stumbled over the bodies of one of my father's section men and two young pioneer settlers who had perished there in the flames," a survivor remembered. "Their clothing had been burned completely off and the bodies were burned almost beyond recognition, in a black, bloated, sickening appearance."[7] One boxcar was about half full of lath; the other was completely loaded with bricks — all for a new house planned by Dr. Kelsey. With the help of the men, the women and children climbed into the car containing the lath. Soon afterwards, a party of twenty-five Russian Jews came up to the car. They had been apart from the main body in the pond, standing up to their necks in the creek and saving themselves by constantly ducking their heads under the water. Those already aboard tried to convince them to go to the second car. The unwanted Jews rejected the uninviting prospect — on top of all their other troubles — of unloading a boxcar full of bricks, ignored the advice, and climbed in with the Christians, finding places as best they could. Dense darkness closed in, relieved only by the flickering light of burning stumps and trees near the tracks.

Lucy found the scene a touching one even for the hardest of hearts: "About forty men, women and children lay stretched on the rough laths, sitting, with weary heads against the sides of the car, or lying at full length upon the floor, so closely packed together that it was impossible to move about without the utmost care. Some of the mothers forgot their little ones, who bravely accepted the situation and dropped off to sleep without pillow or coverlet. Others groaned and caught brief snatches of sleep, wakened by their cramped state of discomfort, to long wakeful hours of misery."[8]

Everyone on No. 45, the Eastern Minnesota accommodation train that jumped the track a few miles to the west of Hinckley, survived the fire. Engineer William Vogel and fireman Joseph Lancher had lain prone on the deck of the cab with the water from the tank turned on them. The rest of the crew and the two passengers fought successfully to save the coaches. Apparently Vogel had run through the cutting edge of the fire before the train wreck; otherwise the wooden coaches would have burned.

Not long after the crew brought the flames in the undercarriages under control, two men supporting one another staggered down the tracks from the direction of Hinckley. The people from No. 45 could hardly believe their eyes: it seemed incredible that anyone from that direction could have lived through the disaster. Both of the men were section hands — Thomas Gorman and his husky young son. The Gorman family had left their small house and sought safety under bridge No. 84, huddling there when the accommodation train passed over and rumbled down the line. They had stayed in the water until the fire passed, then beat out the flames on the bridge, saving the Eastern Minnesota several thousand dollars in property.

Convinced that the train could not have gone much farther without leaving the tracks, Gorman and his son had started in the direction of Pokegama. When the older man tired, the younger helped him the rest of the way to the stricken train. Without any outward display of emotion, the son left the older man beside the train, turned, and walked back up the line to help his mother and the other children in the family. Express messenger John Sanderluis could hardly believe what had happened. He asserted, "The boy after saving the bridge, took his father to the wrecked train and then started right back . . . a deed which not one in a thousand would have done under the circumstances."[9]

About 5:00 p.m., all persons connected with the ill-fated train, except Mr. Gorman, who could not walk, started toward Pokegama. They wanted food and shelter, having no way of knowing that the place had burned to the ground. They were horrified by what they found: the settlement lay in ashes and many citizens had died in the flames. The remains of the railroad bridge, sawmill, and section house were still on fire. The fish in the pond had died. Many of the surviving residents had been burned horribly. "The cries of the children, and the moans and groans of the men and women, were something terrible; pen cannot describe it," John Sanderluis wrote. "The smoke and air were suffocating in the extreme and the heat terrible. We placed wet clothes over their faces and in their mouths every five minutes."[10] Making a quick and decisive decision, E. E. Parr, the conductor, ordered the people to follow him back up the railroad to his train, and they complied without argument. So, the same individuals who had refused to walk in the other direction to the boxcars trooped up the tracks, reaching the train about 7:00 p.m. The crew made them as comfortable as possible under the circumstances. As there were no drugs or food, a long and painful night seemed in prospect.

The sound of a voice startled the refugees crowded into the boxcar full of lath. It was Dr. Kelsey. He appeared, helping two companions who had been with him when the fire struck,

Joe Chipris and M. C. Anderson. "Oh, Uncle," said Maidie Kelsey, "they told us such dreadful things about you." The physician, burned over his back and arms, and with his eyes swollen and nearly blind, thought only of others. Upon learning that his close friend, John Gonyea, lay untended back at the pond, Dr. Kelsey decided to go to his aid. Led by men "who had some use of their eyes," the doctor started up the right-of-way. He returned sometime later with news that Gonyea had decided to remain beside the pond, and that a relief train would come the next morning from Hinckley.

The occupants of the car, believing help on the way, settled down to an uneasy night. At one point the men had to roll out to extinguish a fire in the ties beneath the boxcar, but mainly the people felt uncomfortable and closed in by the cramped quarters. Lucy, feeling oppressed by the atmosphere, got up in the middle of the night and looked out the door. What she saw startled her: "Before me rose a city brilliantly illuminated; some lights low down in basements, others higher; still others in lofty stories; while little points, like electric lights, shone through the seemingly misty air. Over all the silent stars shone with softly tempered radiance. So like lights in city windows, gleaming from afar, seemed those rays from burning tree and stump, and leafless trunk, that I returned to my weary vigil not a little comforted by the weird imagination."[11]

Several miles away at Mission Creek, the fire had consumed twenty-six houses, plus a store, hotel, blacksmith shop, schoolhouse, and station. Thirty-eight farm animals, including twenty-two head of oxen owned by the Laird & Boyle Lumber Co., had perished. However, all seventy-three people lived who had run into the potato field in the rear of the station. For over two hours they had lain flat on the ground, gasping for breath, the heat intense, ashes raining down, and little children crying. After the worst was over, everyone had congregated around a log blockhouse, owned by Swedish immigrant David Heldron, which somehow had survived the conflagration. All concerned felt relieved. The women and children washed their faces. "Several deer were seen running around us [looking] for shelter and one large one got caught on a wire fence and some of the men brought it over to the only house on the place," someone recalled. "We dressed and cooked it and dug up some potatoes and roasted them and partook of supper about 8:20."[12] The ordeal of the Mission Creek residents was nearing its end. Even though they had lost their homes and belongings, they fared better than most of the other people in the fire district. The main force of the fire had missed them, and the heat, while intense, was never strong enough to kill. The Mission Creek residents made it through the blaze by finding safety in the field. Others farther north who took the same action died.

At Hinckley the men, women, and children in the Grindstone River and the gravel pit began to stir. While the remains of the town continued to burn with great force, the Red Demon had passed through, leaving behind unbroken desolation. Of the two places of refuge, the gravel pit had offered the greatest safety. Shallow water covered the bottom of the two- to three-acre community eyesore, some thirty feet below the surrounding country and about three feet deep in the middle. A few trees grew around the pit. The river had trees closely spaced all along its banks. To make matters worse, it was hardly more than a brooklet on 1 September 1894. It contained so little water that at several points it was possible to step across. Under the circumstances, the river proved an uncertain refuge. Father E. J. Lawler and his housekeeper both passed out, only to be revived by the water. Drayman Joseph Tew, his mother, and his oldest girl lay in the water, using old coats to ward off a shower of cinders.[13] Mary McNeil — the older sister of Molly, who escaped on the St. Paul & Duluth train — took her eighty-year-old mother to the river. They had only an apron to throw over their heads. "We stayed in the water about three hours," said Mary. "While we were there we saw several people die around us."[14] Three members of a family of five died before her eyes: "With heartbreaking screams, more like the cries of beasts than human beings, these suffering ones writhed like worms in the mud as they endeavored to find escape from the burning stings of the sparks and of the intense heat." Mrs. Martinson and her five flaxen-haired children had also gone to the river. Her son John said, "I was in the river with my sister. I could swim well. I used to go swimming nearly every day." His sister had yelled, "Come hold me up." Because of the intense heat, he failed to reach her and she slid under the water. Just then, someone yelled, "Go to the pit." John leaped up and ran. "I do not know how I got there," he stated. "I was saved, they died."[15] His mother and the other four children, three girls and a boy, died. A correspondent for the Minneapolis *Tribune* wrote, "They were not touched by flames, but suffered the more merciful death by water."[16] Many others who went to the Grindstone perished, although the exact number was unclear. Most of those who went to the Grindstone did so out of desperation. They did not congregate in any single place, but tried to find a haven at numerous points in the river. Some stayed, either to be boiled alive, asphyxiated, or drowned. Others left. Some made the gravel pit, some dropped from the heat and flames. In the final accounting, the Grindstone River was a killing rather than a saving place.

The gravel pit, large enough to hold all the people present in Hinckley on the day of the fire, contained only about seventy persons when the flames passed over, the reason being that most people who ran to the east side of town made the Eastern Minnesota combination train. Only the remnants had to brave the ravages of the fire from the quarry, among them professional people who had believed that their positions in the community required them to set examples by staying until the very last minute. Mayor Lee Webster, Fire Chief John Craig, and newspaper editor Angus Hay all hunkered down in the water.[17] They barely reached the pit, as did the Reverend Peter Knudsen, the Danish-born pastor of the Hinckley Presbyterian Church, and his wife. As the combination train had loaded, Knudsen had said to his wife, "We are only two. Let us stand together and help these poor women with little children into the train." Just before the train backed north, someone on board had yelled that they had room for two more people. Knudsen had turned to his wife and said, "No, others are left in the village, we must go back if possible and help them to the gravel pit." When they started back into town, they met an overwhelming wave of heat. Mrs. Knudsen, who fell twice, told her husband, "Let us lie down and die together here."[18] Just at that moment, the smoke parted. They saw a wagon and ran to it, rolling underneath, but soon it caught fire. They received a respite, revived, and crept to the gravel pit on their hands and knees, seeking and reaching the water and temporary safety.

One person called the gravel pit "the shadow of a great rock in a weary land"; another thought it a "shelter from the storm."[19]

Several hundred trunks, most left by people who escaped on the Eastern Minnesota train, lined the excavation's west edge. Some individuals drove horses and buggies into the water, while many unattended animals plunged in of their own accord. For the first minutes the ordeal experienced by the people was almost unbearable. "The wind blew direct from the south, and a continual shower of coals and sparks fell on us," editor Hay recorded. "Then began an ordeal of fire lasting about twenty minutes through which I believe few could stand to pass again. It was terrible in the extreme. It was necessary to keep throwing water on the children and it devolved upon very few men to do it. Such a time as that one wishes he had as many arms as an octopus; the Lord knows they could have been used to good advantage. The roar of the storm was so great it was impossible to make one's self heard two feet away. But the wind would carry the almost inaudible mutterings of prayer along to leeward, and the hearers, I think, uttered a silent 'amen.' "[20] Intense heat rolled across, smoke from burning buildings making it impossible to see. As the great tongues of flame flashed overhead, brave men constantly threw water over the women and children. One person died: an unidentified man slipped under the water and drowned without anyone's noticing. The rest made it through the disaster.

Sometime after 7:00 p.m. — no one recorded the exact time — the inmates of the pit realized that, while the remains of the town continued to burn, the heat had obviously lessened. The Red Demon had moved on to the north. Curiously, the survivors thought of food rather than their dead relatives, burned houses, or lost belongings. Some found a number of muskmelons, ate the insides, and used the outside husks for drinking utensils. Mrs. Knudsen discovered a cow and milked it. "Mr. Knudsen and his wife lost their home and all they had which could be lost; but hope, faith, love and character they did not lose," an observer claimed. "Their record is on high and their judgment is with the Almighty who does not forget the deeds of his servants."[21]

Gradually, the people decided to venture out of the gravel pit. Skirting the burning town, they walked about a thousand feet straight south toward the Eastern Minnesota yards and the only structures that appeared to be standing, the railroad roundhouse and the water tank. There, two exhausted men waited: engineer C. P. Fadden and fireman N. Reider. They and Engine

No. 19 had made it through the fire. Their desperate gamble of running south into the conflagration had proved a correct one.[22] Now, they helped those who slowly congregated at the base of the water tower — those from the pit, from the river, from the countryside, from the wells, and from the root cellars. Most could walk, but all were "more or less" injured. Few had any clothes on their backs. The vast majority suffered from smoke inhalation, their eyes smarting painfully. Undeniably, they were fortunate: the blackened bodies of hundreds of other people lay in the burning ruins of Hinckley. Hay reported, "From the roundhouse a good view could be had of the ruins, and though our eyes were sore and swollen from the smoke, heat and sand, and though we gazed on the ruins of home and business, the scene presently was grandly fascinating. It reminded me of the great panorama of the 'Destruction of Pompeii.' The streets looked like some climax in a grand drama, the golden glow from the burning buildings lighting up the scene in a manner strangely grand."[23]

Although someone suggested going to Pine City for help, this was more easily said than done: no one knew if that town existed, and the tracks appeared damaged.

After fleeing the burning station at Miller, conductor Thomas Sullivan, with telegrapher Thompson and his family had staggered north toward Finlayson Depot. It was hard going. By now they were not alone, several people having joined them, including Robert Bell and his fifteen-year-old daughter. Bell, a railroader of long experience, was superintendent and secretary of the Duluth Union Depot and Transfer Company, his primary responsibilities involving station operations. Bell claimed that he had played a major role in saving people on No. 4 by passing out wet towels in the cars, directing people to the lake, and fighting a losing battle to put out fires under the carriages. After that, while carrying his fifteen-year-old daughter, he led a small group of frightened people to the north. Finding a section house, he exclaimed, "Necessity knows no law," broke the latch, and hauled out a handcar.[24] He got the people in it and pumped to Miller Station, arriving shortly before the station burned. There, he and the others left the handcar and proceeded on foot as they did not want to run the risk of being run down by No. 12 way-freight.

A short distance from Finlayson Depot, Sullivan watched as No. 12 appeared out of the distance, slowed, came alongside, and stopped. He ran toward the caboose and shouted, "John, is that you?" Conductor John Roper leaped to the ground and hurried to Sullivan's assistance. Asked where he was going, Roper replied, "I am going to your train." Sullivan answered, "I am afraid you cannot do it." Roper said No. 12 was going to try. Swinging back aboard, he signaled engineer Peter Kelly to get underway. The freight sputtered to life and proceeded on its rescue mission, vanishing into the smoke.

Sullivan and about twenty others gathered at Finlayson Depot. A few were from Finlayson and Miller; the rest had walked from Skunk Lake. When the heat became intense and the roar of the approaching fire grew louder, Sullivan ordered the bedraggled company up the tracks. After walking about two miles to a wide firebreak, they stopped. Sullivan told a companion, "I am afraid we are cut off, as I see fire ahead." Everyone sat down and, after an uneventful hour, they heard a whistle from the south — No. 12 was backing up the railroad. Sheets of flame had made it impossible to go below Miller. Roper stopped at the firebreak, picked up the people, then took his train a mile farther to Rutledge for a brief water stop. Sullivan found the strength to walk to the small station and asked operator Kallis if he had received any word from No. 4. Kallis responded, "Nothing; but they are sending a relief train from Duluth."[25] Sullivan, broken down from exhaustion, collapsed and had to be carried back to the caboose. No. 12 backed another four miles to Willow River, which appeared in no danger. It was twenty-one miles from Hinckley and fourteen from Skunk Lake. After quickly getting the survivors off his train, Roper then signaled "All aboard!" and No. 12 chugged back down the line, hoping that the fire had passed through. "Blackened, blistered, with hair and clothes singed," a reporter said, "they toiled at their heroic work."[26] Again, the train reached Miller, but blazing culverts and trestles made further progress out of the question. With paint burning off the engine, tender, and cars, No. 12 reversed for a second time, returning to Willow River. After observing conditions down the line, the train crew assumed that nobody could possibly have lived through the conflagration. When someone did make it through, they would find only blackened corpses.

☆   ☆   ☆

The combination train on the Eastern Minnesota continued north, puffing into Kerrick for a water stop, thirty-six miles from Duluth-Superior. As William Best oiled his engine, four passengers walked back from the parlor car. "They were very profuse in their expressions of praise and gratitude for all of us," he declared. "They were safe and they knew it, and their relief was great, of course."[27] News agent George Cole also went down to the engine, procured a pail of water, and had time to carry six full pails back to the cars before the train started again.

No. 24 rolled into the West Superior yards about 8:30 p.m. where freight conductor William Campbell officially turned the entire train over to passenger conductor H. D. Powers. Campbell, a stickler for railroad regulations, decided that he did not have the authority to conduct a train beyond the yards. "You will understand, " he explained, "that the trains I ran, Nos. 23 and 24, only run from West Superior to Hinckley and return."[28] This technical point concerned no one except Campbell. In fact, it was irrelevant. Yard workers detached Barry's Engine No. 105 and Best's Engine No. 125, replacing them with switch engines for the trip to the Duluth depot. The brakemen who had ridden through the worst of the fire on Barry's tender required medical attention for their blackened faces. They left the train at West Superior. Both engineers rode on to the station, neither man able to see — both had been temporarily blinded. Best said, "I went home to bed immediately, after bandaging my eyes, to allay the inflammation caused by the heat and smoke. It was 4:00 a.m. before the pain in my eyes would permit me to fall asleep."[29]

By 9:30 p.m., the combination train had reached its final destination. The station was in turmoil. Hundreds of rescue workers and persons seeking information milled around on the platform, while a squad of six police pushed the crowd back so that the refugees could leave the train. After they reached the platform, the police kept them cordoned off. Mayor Ray Lewis of Duluth appeared and gave a short speech welcoming the fire victims to Duluth. Reassuring them that they would receive help, he detailed relief activities. After that, the police led the confused aggregation to the Ideal and Zenith restaurants for "square meals." While they ate, authorities passed among them, asking them to fill out forms and directing them to sleeping quarters.[30] It was a strangely routine and bureaucratic end to an experience that started six hours earlier among the burning buildings of Hinckley.

Few, if any, of the passengers cared about the appropriateness or inappropriateness of the welcome. They worried about friends and relatives, wanted to get back south as quickly as possible, or expressed relief at having escaped with their lives. Minor inconveniences created by well-meaning people caused no concern. Judge Seagrave Smith, later reflecting upon the events in Hinckley, found words unequal to the task. "No pen can adequately describe the awful scene, or the feeling of those who witnessed it," he wrote. "It was an event never to be forgotten. After many stoppings we arrived late in the evening, at Duluth, covered with smoke and dirt, our nervous systems terribly strained, but our lives saved. In that condition we felt happy that we had escaped with our lives and had succeeded in saving many others."[31]

Engineer George Van Pelt had watched from the cab of Engine No. 206 at Dedham as the combination train came up the line. Behind him stretched the cars of extra freight No. 22. The emergency train stopped just long enough for Best to tell Van Pelt about conditions down the line, then it lurched away and roared off. At 8:30 p.m. conductor J. C. Cardle rushed up to the cab with urgent orders that had just come over the wire. They had gone out within minutes after No. 24 reached the yards. The dispatch said that No. 22 should take five boxcars and run down to Partridge to rescue the inhabitants. After Van Pelt opened the throttle, No. 22 plunged into the fire district. Fires burned on all sides, and it was very hot. Going proved slow. Van Pelt frequently had to stop, waiting for his crew to chop burned and fallen trees off the track.[32]

The seventy-three people at Mission Creek finished their late supper of roasted potatoes and venison about the time the combination train reached Duluth. Just as they finished eating, a man appeared out of the smoke, coming from the direction of Pine City. At first they thought it was a rescue worker, but it turned out to be a hiker, twenty-six-year-old John Nelson, on his way to Hinckley, apparently unconcerned about the danger ahead. After indicating that he had seen a work train about two and a half miles south, and promising to ask the station agent at Hinckley to send a relief train to Mission Creek, he strolled casually up the line. Those who watched him go could hardly believe their eyes; the incident seemed unreal. The man disappeared as quickly as he had come, like an apparition in the night.[33]

After Nelson left, the people talked things over and decided that the most logical course was to go to the work train. It seemed pointless to wait for a train that might never come from Hinckley. Traveling in one large group, they started out, went a few hundred feet, and gave up. The night was dark and the ties burned. When no one volunteered to go on, they all turned around and returned to the log hut that had served as their previous refuge. They longed to hear the sound of a train, coming either from the north or the south.

As the air gradually cooled at Skunk Lake, James Lobdell of St. Paul, Holt of Duluth, and Anderson of Minneapolis talked things over. Assuming that Hinckley had been destroyed, the three traveling salesmen decided to go to Pine City for help. Wrapping wet clothing around their feet and ankles and covering their heads with damp coats, they started down the line. Large fires continued to rage out of control and thick smoke filled the air. Stumbling along, the men climbed over fallen telegraph poles and great tamaracks. Between Skunk Lake and Hinckley Big Hill they counted twenty-nine bodies. They waded the Grindstone River, coming upon the remains of more victims — one woman, two men, and two small children. Two hours and forty-five minutes after starting the seven-mile journey, they reached the Eastern Minnesota yards in Hinckley. Feeling unable to continue, Anderson and Holt went to the roundhouse and, without telling who they were, threw themselves on the dirt floor and went to sleep. People in the building assumed they were more refugees from either the river or the pit, and did not disturb them. Gritting his teeth, Lobdell pressed on without stopping. He left the railroad and picked his way through the ashes toward Pine City, burning stumps lighting the route.[34]

At the roundhouse, editor Angus Hay of the *Enterprise* and Carl Veenhoneen felt revived and fit enough to make the trip to Pine City. Five other men helped them find a handcar and wrestle it onto the tracks. "We took a hand-car and started. Our trip was necessarily slow, as the rails were warped in places and we were afraid the culverts were all burned out," Hay reported. "It was my first experience as a pilot on the road, and I confess I know little of the track, but the work was to be done, and it was."[35]

John Stone of Pine City, who represented two St. Paul papers, the *Pioneer Press* and the *Daily Globe*, was a well-known local resident and the proprietor of the Pioneer House, the leading hostelry in town. After waiting all day in vain for hard news from the fire district, he gave up in late evening and wrote a general report for the early editions: "The forest fires north of town are raging with savage fury, the high winds through the day have fanned every spark into a flame and it has been traveling over the country, sweeping everything before it. Settlers are being driven from their homes to seek shelter in the marshes; hay and buildings consumed, and the air in suffocating condition from heat and smoke. The northbound Limited train with all the passengers, is now laid up at this place waiting to get through to Duluth. Crews are out working on burnt culverts and repairing bent rails to get the trains through, if possible, tonight. There is no communication with Hinckley, but it is feared that the town is in imminent danger. Relief crews are being sent out from town as rapidly as possible to aid the distressed settlers. At this writing (10:30 p.m.) the wind has died away and hope has correspondingly increased. No danger to this town at present."[36]

A work train sent out from Rush City to repair a bridge south of Mission Creek had run into intense smoke not far up the line. A mile north of Pine City a section crew had waved their arms, asking for help, but the train did not dare stop — fast passenger

No. 3 was too close behind, if it was on schedule. At Brown's Hill, about eight miles south of Mission Creek, the work train picked up section foreman Gustafson, his crew, his wife, and his two children. Since the situation looked dangerous, the train crew detailed a man to escort the woman and her children back down the track to Pine City. The rest of the section hands climbed on board. A half mile farther on the train reached a bridge threatened by a pile of burning logs. With great difficulty, men moved the timber, saving the structure and making it possible for the train to cross. Engineer Jones ordered section foreman John Powell up onto the front of the engine to act as a pilot. When Powell told him that the men wanted to turn back, the engineer replied that it was as safe to go ahead as to reverse. Five miles south of Mission Creek, foreman Daunchem and his crew, all of Hinckley, flagged down the train, having spent a harrowing time in a creek bottom, cut off by fire on two sides. Next came a burned-out bridge. Powell stayed at the site with five section hands, while the work train backed up rapidly toward Rush City.

Engineer Jones reached Rush City at 6:15 p.m., leaving again at 6:55 with four cars of timber and rails. The crew accomplished a rather remarkable feat in loading the heavy material so quickly. When the train returned to the bridge at 8:00 p.m., bridge foreman John Gillie and his skilled crew went right to work. In fifty minutes the bridge was "rip rapped," enabling the train to cross and move cautiously up the line, until it reached a burned culvert about a quarter mile from Mission Creek. Powell stated, "I rode on the engine and I can tell you we did not know when we might go into the ditch, it was so very dark from smoke, fearfully hot, and we were nearly blinded. Ties were burning all along the line, affording us a little light to see the rails, which in places were badly warped."[37] While a crew repaired the culvert, Powell and a few men went to Mission Creek, where they found the people sheltered in the log hut. Just as workers finished helping them back to the work train, Angus Hay and Carl Veenhoneen arrived on the handcar. At first the two tired men had trouble conveying the magnitude of what had happened in Hinckley. "After considerable talk," said Hay, "we persuaded them to return to Pine City."[38]

After they understood the problem, the train crew acted quickly and with resolution. The work train started the eleven-

mile trip back to Pine City, while Powell and his men continued
to repair the culvert. After finishing, they slowly rode handcars toward Hinckley, repairing "passing track" so that a relief
train could get through. At Hinckley, Powell and the others did
not stop at the roundhouse, proceeding instead to the Grindstone River, where they soon decided the St. Paul & Duluth
bridge would need major repairs to get a heavy train across.
They did not know about the disaster at Skunk Lake. They only
worried about reopening the railroad.

☆   ☆   ☆

James Lobdell staggered into the railroad station at Pine City
at 11:30 p.m., about thirty minutes before the work train returned from Mission Creek. He blurted out shocking news — the
destruction of Hinckley and the flaming wreck of No. 4. The
telegrapher quickly wired J. Michaels, a St. Paul & Duluth official in St. Paul: "Hinckley, Mission Creek, and No. 4 train
are all burned up, except the engine. The passengers on No.
4 train are in Skunk Lake, about six miles north of Hinckley,
and about half the people in Hinckley are dead. We want all
the assistance possible. Notify both doctors at Rush City, and
any others that can be got here at once."[39]
Within minutes, another message hummed down the line.
Correspondent Stone, who had waited hours at the station,
flashed the news to the *Pioneer Press* and *Daily Globe*: "Hinckley burned to ashes; many people lost their lives in the fire,
balance are homeless and destitute; send relief if possible at once.
The little town of Mission Creek entirely wiped out. Engineer
Jim Root probably fatally burned. Situation appalling and heart-
rending in the extreme."[40]
And so, the first hard news of the great calamity in the
pineries reached the outside world. All the trunk telegraph lines
out of Duluth-Superior were disrupted, so there was no traffic
from that direction. At Rush City, Olive Brown, the day operator, who had stayed on duty so that a man could take a night
off, heard the message and hurried immediately to contact the
two physicians. In St. Paul, railroad officials began to plan a
relief train. They placed telephone calls to the mayors of St.
Paul and Minneapolis, the governor of Minnesota, and important business leaders. At the *Pioneer Press* and the *Daily Globe*,
the editors ordered the front page of the morning edition remade

to conform with the new events. A new *Pioneer Press* headline read: "HINCKLEY IN ASHES: Burned in Terrible Forest Fires, and Many Lives Lost."[41] The wire services swung into action. Their reporters in Minneapolis-St. Paul searched for leads that would convey the gravity of a disaster they knew about only in general terms. They realized, however, that they were on to a big national story, one that would grow in importance as more hard news came from northern Minnesota. Newspaper readers around the nation would want to know what had happened.

The unfortunates riding the work train back to Pine City, sleeping in the lath car in Pokegama, sitting in accommodation train No. 45, trying to rest at the roundhouse in Hinckley, standing in the water of the Kettle River, cowering in the cutover near Partridge, felt alone and forgotten. Yet although they did not realize it, people cared about their plight and help was on the way. The survivors' ordeal by fire would end as fast as humanly possible in the United States of 1894.

Chapter 6

"Those Men Are Taking Their Lives in Their Hands"

Pine City hotel owner John Stone, who had sent the first hard news of the disaster to the St. Paul papers, filed another dispatch shortly after midnight: "Relief party has gone from here with medical aid for the suffering and provisions for the hungry. Wires are down and no communication since train came down at 12 o'clock. The town is completely wiped out. The Limited train from Duluth, Root, engineer, was caught in the fire and Root standing to his post like a hero, ran his train back to Skunk Lake with it all on fire, and saved his passengers. When last seen, he was lying in his cab, badly burned but breathing. The people of Mission Creek saved themselves by lying down in a potato patch until the fiery indignation was past. The disaster is full and complete and sad enough to dismay the strongest heart. Relief temporary, substantial, and immediate is needed and needed bad. The Limited passenger train, six miles above Hinckley, is in ashes, and about two hundred people are in the marsh near Skunk Lake, with fire all around them. Yardmaster at Hinckley is badly burned. The relief party is pushing through and hope to get there by 2 o'clock. It was only by the most superhuman effort that the train was backed out of the fire and the passengers saved. Poor Root! he ought to live, such men are always heroes in time of need."[1]

After sending the message, Stone abandoned newspaper reporting and assumed duties as a member of a five-man Pine City relief committee established to aid the Hinckley fire sufferers. Many professional journalists would have considered him a fool: he had first access to a tremendously important national newspaper story, in the parlance of the trade, a real "scoop." Yet Stone felt that he had a more important duty — to aid the survivors of the colossal holocaust.[2]

☆　　☆　　☆

Stone and his fellow relief workers had no way of knowing what was going on north of the fire district because of the downed wires. Duluth authorities had already undertaken a major effort. The hastily converted "Short Line" routed south as a relief train at 7:05 p.m. steamed through increasing concentrations of smoke and cinders, arriving at Willow River after 11:00 p.m.[3] There, the train slowed and came to a stop to the rear of No. 12, the way-freight that had already made two unsuccessful attempts to reach Skunk Lake. Beside the tracks, the railroad men from the two trains held a conference. Yardmaster David Williams, who had brought the special from Duluth, wanted to get to what he called "the front" as quickly as possible. He listened intently as Robert Bell, the Duluth depot supervisor and a passenger on No. 4, said simply that "everything was burned, and everybody dead," and that anyone trying to get through to Skunk Lake "surely would be burned too."[4] The crew of No. 12 told about the problems they encountered.

After hearing the estimates, Williams made a series of decisions. He ordered the fire victims already at Willow River transferred to the relief train. These included the delirious and half-blind conductor Thomas Sullivan. Next, Williams told general agent C. M. Vance to take the train back to Duluth, two of the four medical doctors who had made the down trip, McCormick and Gilbert, going along to tend the sufferers. When the relief train headed north, Williams went south on No. 12, after all except one boxcar had been detached. He had along, in addition to the crew, Superintendent Bell and the other two physicians, Codding and Magie, the latter the railroad's regular surgeon. Again, the train got as far as Miller Station, and again it had to stop. Williams insisted on pressing on. The crew repaired three trestles and succeeded in getting No. 12 over them before a destroyed twelve-foot bridge stopped further progress. Undeterred, Williams had the crew lug a handcar to the other side. He intended to move on to the scene of the tragedy, taking along Bell, conductor John Roper of the way-freight, and the two medical men. The small group, after tying handkerchiefs over their mouths and nostrils, started down the track, disappearing into the burning woods. Pillars of fire from blazing stands of timber cast strange glows through the thick smoke.[5]

James Hurley of Pine City was sitting on a neighbor's front steps, speculating on conditions to the north, when City Marshal J. E. Netser approached and said, "Hinckley is all burned out, and many lives lost." The worst had happened. Hurley went home and told his family. Then, prudently picking a heavy overcoat to use as a defense against falling cinders, he walked downtown to the small park square, where a crowd had gathered. Hurley took charge of relief measures and, without formality, took over as chairman of the hastily formed Pine City Relief Committee. He sent young men and boys off to canvass every house in the village to gather provisions. Within half an hour citizens brought food and liquor to the station. The town's sole physician, Dr. E. E. Barnum, who had no way of knowing whether his daughter Kate had escaped the flames, volunteered his services, as did two medical doctors from the laid-over No. 3 northbound limited. Conductor Buckley of the passenger train, helped by conductor Jim Sargent of the work train, turned part of No. 3 into a special consisting of the engine and two coaches. Posthaste, the train pulled out, leaving the work train behind on a siding, where its four boxcars served as temporary homes for the Mission Creek refugees. Hurley rode the special to Hinckley. He recalled, "We went through fire and smoke, and it was a grand panorama to look upon the flames in the distance, eighty feet high, but dangerous to pass through. I should judge seventy-five men were on the train. On our way we stopped three times to take on hand cars and push cars, to move the sick and the dead."

The train chugged into the south yards in Hinckley sometime between 12:30 a.m. and 1:00 a.m. — no one bothered recording the exact time. By then, about 200 people had gathered in the vicinity of the roundhouse. The doctors immediately started to aid the injured, discovering that almost everyone suffered smoke blindness. Other workers helped people into the coaches. Hurley and a party of volunteers walked up the Eastern Minnesota tracks to the gravel pit, where they found some of the people from the Grindstone River, including Father E. J. Lawler. They carried him and the others, all blinded by the smoke, to the cars. Then, a rescue party hastily searched for survivors in the streets of Hinckley. "With lanterns all adjacent places were reached for the living and the dead," Hurley recounted. "It was a gruesome task, some of them being baked, not yet cold."[6]

Section foreman John Powell returned from reconnoitering

the Grindstone River bridge. He told Buckley, who was in charge, that the structure "was all iron" — the ties had completely burned. Buckley informed him of the plight of No. 4 and said, "Those people are over there, somewhere, and we are bound to get to them."[7] This put the problem in a new perspective for Powell: previously he had thought in terms of opening the line; now he worried about saving lives. After some thought, he said he believed it possible to get handcars over the bridge. After Buckley decided that the plan had merit, he, Powell, Sargent, and seventeen section hands started the difficult task of getting five handcars over the warped rails and on to Skunk Lake. Dr. Barnum went along, as did Angus Hay, both as a rescuer and a newspaper correspondent. While the section hands worked at the river, they could hear the relief train start back to Pine City.

☆   ☆   ☆

The first news of the calamity shocked the residents of Rush City, twenty-three miles south of Hinckley. They knew about the fires to the north. In fact, the local fire department had responded to a call for help from Hinckley earlier in the day by sending 1,000 feet of hose on No. 3 limited. But, no reason existed at that point to believe that Hinckley was in danger of destruction. In any event, the late evening telegram spurred a quick response. The authorities sounded the fire alarm and within minutes an estimated 300 people gathered at the St. Paul & Duluth station. Railroad workers pulled out a light engine which they intended to start north within minutes, carrying physicians J. E. Gemmel and A. J. Stowe, plus five men selected as assistants from the ranks of many volunteers. Those who accompanied the physicians included some of the elite of the town: Mayor S. C. Johnson; attorney and speculator J. D. Markham; Rush City *Post* editor Charles Elmquist; assistant editor Howard Folsom; and school official L. M. Gale. After plans had been formulated to have an impromptu committee gather supplies for a relief train, the party set out. As the party left the depot, a retired railroad man declared in a loud voice, "Those men are taking their lives in their hands."[8] Ahead lay the possibility of burned culverts, downed bridges, and twisted rails.

The "Advanced Guard," as they called themselves, huddled together in the cab, surrounded by medical and other supplies. The engineer opened the throttle wide while the fireman poured on the coal. "The run to Pine City," declared Dr. Stowe, "was made at a speed that was very exciting to say the least."[9] Unfortunately, they arrived after the relief train had left. Railroad officials refused to allow the engine to proceed. With the wires down they could not locate the exact position of the train already north of Pine City, and they would run the risk of either a head-on or rear-end collision. The two physicians tended some of the people from Mission Creek and then waited. After what seemed a lengthy delay, the relief train put together on short notice in Rush City rattled into Pine City. It brought more supplies, several hundred Rush City citizens, Dr. Krogstadt of North Bend, Dr. Tietin of Harris, and — more importantly — several handcars.[10]

Within minutes two handcars started toward Hinckley. While Drs. Stowe, Gemmel, and Krogstadt, plus seven others, rode the first car, Tietin and other members of the Rush City Relief Committee were on the second. The push cars plunged into an inky blackness mingled with fire and smoke — a harrowing journey. "The scene, had there been time to notice it, was one of incomparable grandeur," Dr. Gemmel recounted. "The night was intensely dark; the smoke from the forest fires, which had been raging for days, was almost thick enough to cut with a knife, and the lanterns on the cars only served to light for a short distance ahead 'the straight and narrow way' over which the pioneers were traveling. It was too dark to distinguish the forest on either side of the track, but with every rod traveled could be seen in the distance 'as through a glass dimly' the light of a burning tree. Very often the fire would be seen suspiciously close to the track, and, to the anxious eyes of those who were in advance, appeared to be the red light of an approaching train. Then the speed would slacken and a flagman sent ahead to investigate."[11]

A short distance out of Mission Creek the handcars met the relief train backing from Hinckley to Pine City. The train stopped well before any danger of an accident. After a hasty discussion, Mayor Johnson, Dr. Stowe, and Dr. Krogstadt climbed aboard the Pine City train. Severely burned people needed attending and someone had to help coordinate hospital activities in Pine City. The rest of the group went on to Hinckley, where they helped eight to ten people suffering from the effects of the fire. Dr. Gemmel diagnosed their "principal trouble" as coming from smoke and damage to their eyes.[12]

George Van Pelt sat at the throttle of Engine No. 206 as freight No. 22 edged south from Dedham toward Partridge. About 1:00 a.m., he reached a bridge approximately half a mile above Partridge. As it appeared unsafe and flames rose from the woods on both sides of the track, Van Pelt decided not to go onward. Just as he prepared to reverse, some people ran up to the engine and said that many refugees had gone to a lake some distance from the line. Backing up slowly, Van Pelt sounded his whistle over and over. At a logging road a great number of persons appeared and climbed into the five freight cars. They came from Partridge and the surrounding countryside. Roaring flames, swirling smoke, stifling heat, and the movement of the train impeded rescue operations. "We got all but three or four people, who were overcome with heat and gave up, so they could not be saved," Van Pelt stated. "All told we brought about two hundred refugees in on our train."[13] He wished he had made it all the way to Hinckley, but at least he had the satisfaction of knowing that he succeeded in bringing a large number of people to safety from the fire district.

At the Kettle River the survivors gradually stirred to life. The worst appeared over; an occasional flash gave the only indication of fire. Most people were cold; many had spent several hours standing in the water. Patrick Regan, one of the strongest, decided to look for a place of refuge. "I discovered an old powder house in which were four large kegs of powder," he claimed. "I picked up an old empty powder can, filled it with water and threw it upon the burning sticks which were lying about. I made everything safe outside, then went in and carried out the powder kegs and threw them into the river. I then wet the floor of the powder house so that there might not be any danger there." He helped many women and children to the powder house. Although a couple of men went inside and refused to come out, the rest remained outside. A small number went to Sandstone to see what had happened. What they found shocked them: nothing remained but a few smoking tree limbs and half-charred bodies. The disconsolate group returned to the river. "We found a half-burnt boat by the river side, which we made use of as a kind of shelter against the raging whirlwind of sand and ashes," the Reverend E. Anderson commented. "Thus, we remained during the night." An old man recalled, "It was a horrible, a terrible night. May I be spared living through another one like it."[14]

Below the burning Kettle River bridge, Eastern Minnesota watchman M. W. W. Jesmer stood in the water throughout the night with his wife and four children. Two other people had joined them, Thomas McCoy and Nels Flygt. The deep water close to the edge of the river forced the small group to struggle to keep from drowning. After the fire passed the only sound that they heard was the mournful howling of a dog.[15]

Over eighty miles to the south of the Kettle River, a special train highballed out of the St. Paul & Duluth yards in St. Paul. Besides the engine, it had a baggage car and a coach. Back in the coach, L. S. Miller, the railroad's assistant manager and road-master, sat with his staff. Not waiting for any relief supplies — they could follow later — he hurried to the fire district as quickly as the wheels would turn. He knew nothing about the conditions on the railroad, except that No. 4 had apparently been destroyed. He intended to learn what he could and take charge of operations. Given the downed wires, he felt the only logical course was to go directly to the scene. He needed hard information to plan relief activities and to get the railroad back into normal operation.[16]

The handcar carrying Yardmaster David Williams and the others in his small party inched south down the warped tracks from Miller to Skunk Lake, feeling their way along. The wood-work in the culverts and bridges had all burned away. On some stretches the railroad ties had turned to ashes. At times, the group had to leave the handcar and manhandle it over ravaged sections of the track. They gradually moved along, counting eighteen bodies, all burned beyond recognition. Six children numbered among the dead. Someone found a lady's traveling bag of an older style. Absent-mindedly, he tossed it on the car, not learning until later that the contents included $3,500 in negotiable certificates of deposit belonging to fire victim Mrs. John McNamara.

About 3:00 a.m. the handcar reached Skunk Lake. Except for the crackling flames from the coal in the tender of Engine No. 69, they heard no sound. Superintendent Robert Bell commented, speaking to no one in particular, "Can it be they are all dead?" Williams seemed resigned to failure, believing everyone had perished. For a while, they just stood, not knowing exactly what to do next — look for bodies in the dark or go back and report the tragedy. Bell suggested, "Let us holler."[17] They did in unison, shouting "Hallo! Hallo!" To their astonishment a great chorus of voices answered. Many people had survived in the mud and slime of Skunk Lake, but they had not heard the rescue party arrive. Williams and Bell rushed toward the first men who appeared from the lake. Senator Frank Daugherty, businessman William Blades, and porter John Blair shook the two railroad officials' hands. Daugherty had led his son and the women they helped back to the swale from the potato patch. Blades, after spending several hours in the water, had experienced the sensation of severe heat giving way to extreme cold. He felt as though he was standing in a "raw winter wind."[18] Blair, a tower of strength throughout the ordeal, had attended "strictly to business," cheerfully and confidently predicting to the anguished victims that "it would soon be over."[19] Now, the end was near.

After Blair gave a candid account of what had happened, indicating the passengers were safe, Williams saw no need to stay at the wreck. They quickly rejected as impractical the idea of having everyone who could stand walk back to Miller Station. The two physicians, Magie and Codding, remained at the scene, while Williams and the others in the original party started immediately for Miller. After they arrived, Williams put all available men to work opening the line to Skunk Lake. He personally supervised operations.

Williams scribbled a message to Duluth for Bell to take back to Rutledge station. Telegrapher Kallis sent it humming up the wire to Duluth. It stated: "Have been to wreck with handcar — could only get to Miller by train. Wreck is one and one-half miles south of Miller and burned up — passengers all right but exhausted — they are in a marsh — we go with timber to build bridge — tell everyone all are alive and well as can be expected — will arrive in Duluth at 9:00 a.m."[20] The telegram arrived in Duluth in garbled form. The transmission had not made it clear whether the people were dead or saved. By now it was about 3:45 a.m. The "Short Line" relief train sent out to Willow River had just backed into the Duluth depot. After consultation, railroad officials decided not to send it back out. Rather, they started to plan a more extensive effort for the daylight hours.

Authorities made arrangements to have the Partridge refugees housed and cared for in Superior. When George Van Pelt eased No. 22 freight to a halt in the West Superior yards, a great many carriages waited alongside the tracks. The fastest rushed the most seriously burned directly to the hospital, while the rest carried the other survivors to the Superior City Hall, which served as a processing center. As emergency workers distributed food and clothing, clerks assigned quarters either in hotels or boarding houses.[21]

Section foreman John Powell had succeeded by 2:30 a.m. in getting five handcars across the badly burned St. Paul & Duluth bridge over the Grindstone River. "At times it seemed impossible to get across, the heat was so intense, and the bridge so long, with the mill burning so near," he explained. After experiencing more trouble on Hinckley Big Hill, the relief party started its run, contending all the way with burned ties and warped rails. Three miles north of Hinckley, a badly burned man staggered along the track. As only part of his underwear remained, the section men gave him some of their clothing. A quarter mile from Skunk Lake the caravan reached a burned-out culvert. While the crew repaired the damage, Powell, with the two conductors, Buckley and Sargent, picked their way to the wreck. Climbing into the engine cab, they found engineer James Root propped up on the floor. Powell said, "Hello, Jim! How do you feel?" Root answered, "I am poorly," but showed no sign of recognition. He had a wet towel pressed against his

forehead. One of the conductors said, "We have a doctor, Jim."
The other sadly commented in a low voice, "A doctor is no good,
now!"[22] He underestimated the engineer.

Root, after all he had gone through during the previous
several hours, was determined to live. After lying for more than
four hours in the water, he had pulled himself onto the bank.
When feeling had gradually returned to his numbed body, he
started to shiver. Turning to fireman McGowan, he declared,
"I am going to get warm somehow. I am going back to the
engine." McGowan told him, "You can't live on the engine for
the coal is on fire."[23] Still, McGowan helped his engineer into
the cab, even making an unsuccessful attempt to shovel the
burning coals out of the tank. A compassionate passenger gave
Root a towel. When the Duluth vanguard arrived, Root briefly
considered going with them to Miller but decided he was too
weak. After Powell, Buckley, and Sargent arrived, he started
to feel much better. He got up, climbed down from the cab,
and walked to a handcar, which had just reached the scene after
crossing the repaired culvert. He wanted to go home to White
Bear.

Buckley and Sargent distributed to the survivors milk, water,
bread, and "stimulants" that they had brought along. Many
eagerly drank the "balm of comfort" from a fifteen-gallon coal
oil can.[24] When Powell started north on a handcar carried
around the wreck, he discovered people all along the right-of-
way. He found his friend McNamara, a section foreman from
Hinckley, standing as if in a daze. Farther on he encountered
three salesmen, one of whom wandered aimlessly with no
apparent purpose. After deciding that there was nothing he
could do, he sent the handcar on to meet No. 12 and returned
to Skunk Lake.[25]

In Duluth, J. L. Greatsinger, president and general manager
of the Duluth and Iron Railway, had spent most of the night
at the Spalding Hotel, consoling people with friends and relatives
on No. 4. After several hours passed, it became apparent that
the St. Paul & Duluth intended to do nothing more until
morning. Greatsinger, after considerable thought, suddenly had
an idea. He turned to a companion and exclaimed, "It does not
seem right that no effort is being made to reach the women and

children at the point where the limited train burned. If we were
in the same place, it would cheer us to know that our friends
were making an endeavor to reach us. If you will go with me
I will get an engine and car and we will start tonight."[26] When
the man nodded agreement, they both walked to the dispatcher's
office on the St. Paul & Duluth Railroad. Greatsinger demanded
the "rights of the road" and a train. The dumbfounded night
dispatcher quickly honored his request: railroad presidents —
even those from other roads — were not men to be ignored.
While Greatsinger's railroad was relatively short — it
transported ore from the range to the docks of Duluth-Superior
for shipment to eastern mills — the line constituted an important
component of the iron and steel industry. So, workers pulled
out an engine and coach and switched Greatsinger's opulent
private car from the Duluth and Iron Railway to the St. Paul
& Duluth, attaching it to the train. By 5:30 a.m. what qualified
as a "silk stocking" relief train rolled out of the depot, moved
through the yards, and steamed down the line. It contained
important Duluth citizens, but no physicians or medical
supplies. Greatsinger, in keeping with the expected image of
a railroad tycoon, ignored that he was not running over his own
tracks or that the crew worked for someone else. He took charge
of the short train and no one questioned his right to do so.[27]

About 6:00 a.m., No. 12 — on its third attempt — reached
Skunk Lake. The most logical course, the one they adopted,
was to send as many people as possible south on the handcars
to Hinckley and to take the rest north to Duluth. Within a short
time the necessary arrangements were made. No. 12 backed up
the line at a slow speed, carrying roughly 200 people, while
the handcars pumped back south with another forty survivors.[28]
Except for a few railroad workers who remained to plan track-
clearing operations, Skunk Lake was again just another
insignificant marsh along the Duluth & St. Paul main line. None
of the passengers on No. 4 or the Hinckley refugees regretted
leaving, yet they all realized that the uninviting spot had saved
their lives.

Section hands connected the handcars with planks in order to accommodate more people. They took out seriously injured individuals, women and children, and some influential personages, C. D. O'Brien one of the latter. He had not pulled any strings; someone recognized him and ushered him to a handcar. As the handcars moved along, the state of the country shocked O'Brien, and he found what he saw difficult to describe: "Before the fire it had been covered with a heavy growth of small trees, principally poplars, birch, and tamarack; here and there among them were a few larger trees, and some of the older stumps were standing, but from Skunk Lake, where we had stopped, to the bridge at Hinckley and as far as could be seen on each side of the track the ground was swept as with a broom of fire; no vestige remained of the railroad fences, very little of the telegraph poles, a small number of these latter standing in some instances; and the herbage and foliage were absolutely swept from the ground. So great had been the heat that the ties were charred and burned, the rails in many places twisted so out of shape that the handcars had to be lifted around them, and the sides of the cuts presented a baked and calcined appearance; the bodies of deer and rabbits lay along the track, and when some two miles and a half from Hinckley we came across the first human bodies the full horror of the situation was apparent to us. Between the point where we stopped and the bridge at Hinckley on the road side inside the right of way and along the road were some twenty-two bodies, some in groups of three or four, others singly, burned to a crisp and some of them partially consumed."[29]

Dr. A. J. Stowe of Rush City, who had left a handcar to join the train backing from Hinckley to Pine City, found deplorable conditions among the refugees. "I do not know how many the train held, but there must have been at least one hundred and fifty persons, all suffering from the effects of heat and smoke, and many from the effects of severe burns, all blackened beyond recognition," he remembered. "As yet, nothing had been done to speak of to relieve the suffering, which was intense."

By the time the train returned to Pine City, local residents, along with those who had arrived on the Rush City train, had turned the skating rink into a hospital. At this "Rink Hospital," the work of washing wounds and applying dressings began in earnest. Dr. Stowe said, "Several were so badly burned that their lives were despaired of. No fewer than a fourth were quite severely burned about the hands, feet and head, and all were suffering from pain in the lungs and eyes, the effects of heat and inhaling the smoke." Volunteer nurses did all they could to aid the "half burned and totally despairing creatures."[30] While some succored the sick, others served milk brought in from Rush City, the work continuing well into the morning hours. "In less than twenty-four hours after the disaster," the editor of the Pine City *Pine County Pioneer* reported, "the whole of the village was turned into an immense boarding house, meals being served in the K of P hall and the courthouse was converted into a sleeping chamber while those that were injured were taken to the old skating rink . . . where they were made as comfortable as possible."[31]

Soon after daylight the train returned to Hinckley, after remaining only a short period in Pine City. It carried disaster workers and supplies from Pine City and Rush City. At about the same time, the handcars arrived from Skunk Lake. Understandably, there was feverish activity, people running to and fro, performing errands of mercy.

Dr. J. E. Gemmel of Rush City had worked constantly since reaching Hinckley during the night by handcar. Mostly, he treated people with smoke- or fire-damaged eyes. At dawn, taking a short respite, he walked outside the Eastern Minnesota roundhouse and surveyed the desolation. "The coal in the sheds where the depot once stood was blazing fiercely, while on the other side of the track and close to the bridge, piles upon piles of lumber were burning. Thick, dense clouds of black smoke filled the air and myriads of sparks were borne northward on the morning wind. Looking northeast from the Eastern Minnesota round house, not a vestige could be seen of what was, a day before, a fair and flourishing town. Nothing but ashes, smoke and flame met the eye. Even the very dust in the streets was burnt by that terrible fire. The horror deepened on closer inspection. At almost every step through the place one would see some sight evidencing the awful fatality. The bodies of the men, women and children were found on every side, mingled often in a confused mass with dead animals. The sight was one utterly impossible to describe or imagine, and one which, once seen, could never be forgotten."[32] Yet with the dawn came renewed hope. The twin ordeals of fire and darkness had ended. Relief and reconstruction lay ahead.

Chapter 7

"Aren't You Glad to See Somebody?"

A beautiful blue dawn broke over Minnesota on Sunday, 2 September 1894. It promised the kind of day normally associated with late summer in the Upper Midwest — crisp and clear with a low sky. A pleasant, moderate wind blew away much of the heavy haze that had hung for days over the state. Only one thing marred the picture: some of the most productive areas of northern Minnesota lay in burning and smoking ruins. There was no way of telling how many had died.

Tams Bixby, the private secretary of Governor Knute Nelson of Minnesota and an important Republican politician in his own right, knew that a busy day lay ahead of him. His boss had just told him to coordinate relief activities, giving him fifteen minutes to put a plan into operation — a job more easily directed than accomplished on a Sunday morning. He would have to contact people of importance in the community, almost all of whom would be attending church. Bixby realized, however, that he had no choice but to go to work, and that he had behind him the full dignity and majesty of the executive branch of the state of Minnesota. Picking up his telephone, he called the Minnesota National Guard, reaching a captain on Sunday duty. After explaining the seriousness of the situation to the officer and asking for tents, Bixby learned to his frustration that the Guard had taken almost all the canvas they owned to the annual encampment at Salt Lake City. After making arrangements to have it shipped home, Bixby placed a series of calls to wholesalers in St. Paul, asking them to bring food and supplies to the railroad station. He already knew that the St. Paul & Duluth planned to send a relief train. Unfortunately, he had no knowledge of what the people in the fire district needed.[1] A telegram he sent to State Senator Fred A. Hodge in Pine City, "What is needed? Answer quick," received no immediate reply.[2] With little to go on, Bixby went ahead preparing for the relief train, which he hoped to have on the way north by mid-afternoon.

Over a thousand miles from the fire district, a large and muscular middle-aged man registered deep concern as he read the first fragmentary dispatches about the fire. James J. Hill, sitting in his private car on a Great Northern siding in Helena, Montana, had reason for worry: the famous "Empire Builder" owned the Eastern Minnesota Railway, and he stood to lose millions of dollars in property. Yet, despite his Robber Baron image, he thought of the thousands of distressed people who had lost their homes and loved ones. Wiring his assistants in Minneapolis, he instructed them to make "liberal donations" of money in his name and to do everything possible for the sufferers. With the preliminaries out of the way, Hill ordered his private train back to Minnesota. Always a man of action, he wanted to reach the scene of the calamity.

At Duluth, his son, James Norman Hill, started south early in the morning on a special Eastern Minnesota work train, taking with him Superintendent M. V. S. Thome and Road Master Deviny, plus other railroad officials and workers. The son, not thinking as altruistically as the father, took no relief supplies along. He was making the trip merely to ascertain the extent of damage to the railroad.[3]

Mayor William H. Eustis of Minneapolis read the front page of the Sunday morning *Tribune* with more than usual interest, feeling a need to know more about the fires sweeping the northern parts of the state. The banner headline caught his attention: "INFERNO IN FORESTS! Northern Wisconsin and Northeastern Minnesota in Flames. Many Towns Are Wiped Out of Existence and Much Property Destroyed. Scores, Perhaps Hundreds of Lives Have Been Sacrificed in the Great Holocaust." The ensuing article provided only a general account: "The fire demons which lurk in the forests at this time of year are running riotous throughout the great timber country and residents have lost all control. . . . Accurate information as to the location of the fires or their dimensions cannot be obtained for miles and miles of telegraph wire is lying in molten pools on the ground, so intense was the heat of the flames. . . . Some fires have been burning for a month, but they attained no unusual proportions until yesterday morning, when a high wind arose and fanned them into fury. Everybody turned out to check their advance, but the task proved too great. The half-charred timber burned like tinder and the wind carried the mischief to new sections. Some gloomy reports are expected today." Unspecified sources claimed that Hinckley and Mission Creek had "gone up in smoke," with fifty presumed dead.[4]

The fragmentary news tended to confirm what Mayor Eustis had heard earlier — a massive calamity had occurred in the woodlands. He had a reputation as a humanitarian. A soup kitchen that he had established the previous winter to serve the needy of Minneapolis exemplified his desire to have his administration help the poor and unfortunate. He wanted to aid the fire victims, but, as a practical consideration, he determined that he could not do much on a Sunday morning, except make plans and obtain more information. He began calling merchants in anticipation of a relief train, and he summoned his private secretary, J. T. Mannix. Eustis told him to represent the city and to take the first train possible to the fire district.[5] Next, the mayor sent a telegram to State Senator Hodge: "You have the unmeasured sympathy of our people in your terrible affliction. Will rush relief: hope to send car of provisions in a few hours. Do you need any medical help? Wire for anything specific you need at once."[6]

Express messenger John Sanderluis of the wrecked Eastern Minnesota accommodation train No. 45 spent a restless and sleepless night, the cries of the children and the moans and groans of the adults keeping him awake. At dawn he started for Hinckley with engineer William Vogel, fireman Joseph Lancher, conductor E. E. Parr, and theatrical agent Kingsley. "The smoke was still suffocating, and we had to fill our mouths with waste which we had to dip from a pail of water," Sanderluis recalled. "The first thing we found on arriving at Hinckley was about one hundred and fifty cars of wheat burning, which gave out such a heat that we had to avoid it, by at least two blocks to the south."[7] The roundhouse, coal shed, and water tank were the only structures standing; everything else had burned to the ground. Rescue workers gave the No. 45 survivors some bread and crackers. When a man appeared with a cow, Parr obtained permission to milk her. He and the rest sat down and waited for a relief train. Thanking God that they were alive, they resigned themselves to having to return home to St. Cloud via Minneapolis-St. Paul.

The people west of Pokegama in the lath car welcomed the dawn, hoping it was a harbinger of speedy relief. Some individuals carted pails of water for drinking, bathing, and wetting eye bandages. Resourceful Russian Jews found potatoes, eggs, and cabbages for breakfast. When a few persons complained about the quality of the fare, someone retorted, "We ought to be thankful that we have any breakfast at all." The majority chimed, "Indeed, we should."

Dr. C. A. Kelsey, incapacitated by his burns, suggested that someone should go to John Gonyea, lying on the ground back by the pond. When none of the men volunteered, Lucy Kelsey made up her mind to try. Before anyone could stop her, she climbed down from the boxcar and started up the track, feeling in no danger. After all, no fast limited trains or hurtling freights would come charging along the tracks. Lucy quickly learned a good way to make fairly fast progress. She looked ahead, then covered her face with a cloth and walked along blind until feeling a need to check for further pitfalls. She eventually reached the ruins of Pokegama: "When opposite our settlement I found it impossible to locate any house in that direction. At last, as I neared the ruined trestle, I saw what I knew must be the ruins of the mill, smoking and blazing as well. Further on a pile of sawdust was sending up a dismal volume of smoke, and taking my bearings by these, I crossed over and passed in the vicinity of where the stables had stood. A great ox lay turned on one side, and as the creature seemed not to be burned, even slightly, I concluded that it had suffocated."

She found Gonyea, completely covered with quilts, sleeping soundly. "Good morning," she said. "Is there anything I can do for you?" The startled Gonyea woke and mumbled, "I think not, unless you can find something for me to eat. I have had nothing since yesterday morning." Lucy replied, "I am quite sure I can." She went to the smoking foundations of the Baty house, where she found crackers, biscuits, and potatoes, the latter which she ingeniously roasted in the burning roots of an old stump. When a man from the lath car appeared about the time the breakfast finished cooking, he helped Lucy feed Gonyea. They bound the unfortunate victim's hands and feet with makeshift bandages of scraped potatoes. Leaving him covered with wet quilts, they walked back to the car. "The sorrowful sight of his hands and feet, blackened and blistered, with skin peeling off," Lucy asserted, "helped me to realize the suffering I and my dear ones had been spared."[8]

The morning sun at Sandstone looked down upon what the Reverend Emil Anderson called "the black desert of destroyed homes." He and others walked up from the river to the town. "Here lay scattered all about, the burnt corpses of my beloved friends," Anderson recounted. "Amongst these I recognized some of my own church-members, and about half the children who used to attend our Sunday-school. Almost ten feet from her own house a mother was found, burnt to a black corpse, with her two little children by her side, one under each arm. The feeling I had, confronted with this sight, cannot be translated into words. Tears drowned the power of utterance, and not a word could I speak."[9] Axel Friesendahl, who disobeyed his father and went up to the town, noted that nothing remained of Sandstone, only a few tree stumps smouldered. The flames had consumed everything else.[10]

Most people dug and ate already-roasted potatoes, their first nourishment in twenty-four hours. When someone found three cows and a calf standing in the river, they slaughtered the calf and milked the cows, providing food and milk for the babies. Someone discovered a few dead hogs, and salvaged cooked meat from the burned carcasses. Two men struck out across country to Hell's Gate, a "boarding house" on the St. Paul & Duluth Railroad, between Miller and Finlayson. They found that the "girls" at the establishment had a considerable quantity of provisions. After they returned to the river, a group of survivors, including Anderson, decided to go there, despite the place's unsavory reputation. The weakest made the trip in a wagon pulled by two horses found in the water. When the wayfarers passed through Sandstone, many became nauseated. At Hell's Gate they washed, enjoyed a hearty dinner, and went to bed. Anderson estimated the time as about 1:00 in the afternoon.[11]

☆   ☆   ☆

An abnormal level of special railroad activity occurred on Sunday morning. J. L Greatsinger's silk-stocking train chugged into Rutledge at 10:00 a.m., having made slow progress because of frequent stops to check the condition of bridges. There, it met No. 12, returning from Skunk Lake. After the transfer of some persons from the grubby boxcars to the comfortable coaches, Greatsinger reversed his train. Yardmaster Williams, also aboard, wanted to make up a wrecker to clear the tracks at Skunk Lake and send an engine and crew down from Carlton to repair the telegraph lines. He left section foreman John Powell, who had come to Rutledge on No. 12, temporarily in charge of repair operations. Several hundred men and women were waiting in the Duluth depot when the silk-stocking train arrived at 12:15 on Sunday afternoon. Rumors that eight bodies would be unloaded proved unfounded. Instead, as a reporter stated, "A few injured people were brought on the train, but none were seriously hurt," with only one exception.[12]

James J. Hill's son-in-law, Samuel Hill, who by coincidence had the same last name, was president of the Eastern Minnesota. He had gone south with Greatsinger, planning to walk to Sandstone. After a short distance, they decided they had no reason to continue: the situation looked hopeless. Everything had been burned and the ashes were still hot. So, they turned back to Rutledge, planning to wait for the wrecker and go on to Hinckley, hoping to get to Sandstone from that direction. Meanwhile, James Norman Hill had also been thwarted in an attempt to reach Sandstone. When his work train reached Partridge, burned bridges and twisted track stretched ahead. He led a party as far as the destroyed Kettle River bridge, took in the situation, and went back to his train. He instructed the engineer to reverse to West Superior, assuming Sandstone had been wiped out.[13]

South of Hinckley, Pine City and Rush City became centers of relief activities. The first rescue train to reach Hinckley shuttled back and forth from the ill-fated town to Pine City, the location of the temporary Rink Hospital. At Rush City, L. S. Miller, the St. Paul & Duluth official who rushed through the night on a hastily made-up special to Pine City, began the difficult task of getting the railroad back in operation; he could only assume that others were doing the same thing from the

Duluth end. In St. Paul, top St. Paul & Duluth managerial personnel boarded the regular Sunday morning passenger train to Duluth, planning to take it as far north as possible. Although it carried no physicians or relief supplies, the train did have some revenue passengers, including Judge J. C. Nethaway of Stillwater, Minnesota. Nethaway, returning from a western trip, heard about the fire while changing trains in St. Paul. Wanting to help — and possibly to advance his political fortunes — he bought a ticket and had no trouble boarding the northbound train. At White Bear, not far out of St. Paul, the train stopped and did not continue. Miller had halted all traffic, intending to run a special hospital train south as soon as it could be put together and loaded.[14]

Mayor Ray Lewis of Duluth, the first important public official intimately involved with relief activities, responded promptly. Upon learning Saturday evening about the combination train on the Eastern Minnesota, he had taken emergency measures to provide food and shelter for the victims. Although his speech of civic welcome at the station may have been inappropriate and his use of the police to cordon off and herd survivors to eating places may have smacked of totalitarianism, he had acted swiftly and effectively. Planning ahead, he saw the need to mount a massive community effort to help the victims. Realizing the difficulties inherent in gaining widespread support on a Sunday morning, he used the best means available, the Duluth *News Tribune*. At his request, a "Proclamation" issued by his office appeared on the front page of the Sunday morning edition: "A meeting of the businessmen and citizens of Duluth will be held at the council chamber in the city hall at 11 o'clock this morning for the purpose of appointing a relief committee to provide ways and means for the care of the people who have been left destitute and homeless by the disastrous fire, which has burned so many flourishing neighboring towns. Hundreds of men, women and children were brought to the city last night and are in the armory and lodging houses down town, who have lost their all and are scantily clothed. We must provide food and clothes for them at once. The occasion demands immediate action and I feel assured that there will be a hearty response to this call."[15] The mayor placed the gravity of the situation ahead of the morning calls to worship.

When the well-attended meeting opened, Mayor Lewis briefly outlined what had happened, emphasizing the scope of the tragedy. He said 1,000 refugees already were or shortly would be in Duluth. He defended the use of the police, noting that no relief agencies existed to deal with mass suffering. At his urging, the participants in the proceedings established what by degrees grew into the Citizens' Central Relief Committee. During its first hours of operation it received approximately $4,000 in subscriptions. Ultimately, the organization appointed a series of subcommittees to deal with transportation, finance, lumber and general supplies, quarters and commissaries, identification and adoption, auditing, insurance loans, clothing, and widows and orphans.[16] Although Mayor Lewis did not serve as chairman of the central committee, he pulled enough political strings so that he exercised overall control.

The occupants of the lath car near Pokegama started to count their losses and their blessings. All the members of the two Kelsey families lived through the fire. Joe Chipris and M. C. Anderson survived by hiding in a stream with Dr. C. A. Kelsey. Even though he sustained severe burns, John Gonyea lived by lying flat in a small pool. The two older Bramans were safe. John Powers, William Thompson, and Frank Lepengraver saved themselves in a meadow. Joe Frame was alive, and so were numerous others. But, many people numbered among the missing. No one had seen Jakey Braman since his father left their rig at the start of the fire. The Raymonds, Molanders, and Charles Andersons had not appeared, nor had two brothers, James and Robert Barnes. Albert Whitney was gone. Given the conditions, it appeared that they had all perished in the flames. Mrs. Braman cried, realizing the inevitable. "Poor, tearful, heartbroken mother, her fears were too well grounded!" wrote Lucy Kelsey. "Vainly we tried to comfort her, and bade her hope, feeling in our hearts, even before we knew with certainty, that hopes were vain."[17] Punctuating the futility of hoping for the best, someone appeared with news that the Molanders all lay dead, burned to cinders along with their farm.

☆   ☆   ☆

The hamlet of Mora, twelve miles west of Pokegama on the Eastern Minnesota, had escaped what the editor of the Mora *Kanabec County Times* later called "a devilish incarnate fiend" of a fire "driven forward by a tornado."[18] The small community lay only a mile or so west of where the Red Demon started to sweep through the forests. Yet no one in Mora had any inkling of the great disaster so close to their doors, not a single resident bothering to walk up the track to check the countryside. Even the fact that no trains came through after No. 45 rattled east failed to arouse interest. Those who thought about it concluded that the downed telegraph wires and the heavy smoke cover had curtailed railroad operations. On Sunday morning, Anton Smith arrived in town, having walked overland from Pine City. He gave a general outline of the destruction of Hinckley, and at first no one believed him. It took a while for the terrible truth to sink in. After it did, the town organized a relief expedition. Ole Nelson, the section foreman, took his crew and started toward Pokegama on a handcar, not knowing what to expect. About noon, they came alongside the lath car, stopped, and handed out bread, meat, and other food. "Aren't you glad to see somebody?" one of the section hands inquired. "Indeed we are," came the universal reply.[19] The handcar pumped on to Pokegama and picked up John Gonyea. Two men from the lath car, William Thompson and Frank Lepengraver, joined the handcar on its return trip to Mora. Although uninjured, they both were through with Pokegama. They wanted to get away from the fire district.[20]

People in St. Cloud had sensed on Saturday that something was wrong to the east in the pineries. Unverified reports claimed that a massive forest fire raged. In mid-afternoon, after Eastern Minnesota officials received reports of downed bridges, they sent out a large work train carrying forty men and heavy water barrels. It returned about 9:00 p.m., stopped twenty miles up the line by burned ties, downed telegraph wires, and thick smoke. After ordering a regularly scheduled eastbound train carrying about fifty passengers to lay over in St. Cloud, the yardmaster made preparations to dispatch a larger and better-equipped work train at first light. Not knowing the whereabouts of accommodation train No. 45, he assumed it had laid over somewhere until the smoke cleared and crews repaired the track.

On Sunday morning, concern heightened. No telegraph transmissions came from the east; those from Minneapolis-St. Paul were garbled and made little sense. One dispatch seemed to mention a relief train. After being alerted by the railroad, Mayor D. W. Bruckart of St. Cloud talked things over with some members of the council and then scheduled a mass meeting for Sunday afternoon at the Grand Central Hotel. The "largely attended" gathering had an important result: the city decided to sponsor a relief train. It had learned enough to warrant prompt action on relief measures. However, the train could not be dispatched immediately. Railroad officials reported the damage to the line even more serious than expected. They issued a call for all available men, and made up two additional work trains.[21]

Two young men, Peter Nyberg and Gus Johnson, walked toward Mission Creek. On Saturday they had left the small settlement to go haying. When the fire came they had gone to a creek, experiencing little discomfort. They considered the sudden rush of flames a routine part of living in northern Minnesota. The rest of the day was a lark. With the hay burned, they simply sat back and enjoyed themselves, going ahead with a previously formulated plan to spend the night in the wilderness. Sunday morning they walked back to Mission Creek, and what they found shocked them. There was only desolation and not a person to be seen. Only after the relief shuttle picked them up did they learn the scope of the disaster and the good news that friends and relatives had made it through relatively unscathed.[22]

The St. Paul & Duluth relief train left the St. Paul Union Station early on Sunday afternoon. The vanguard of many more, it carried food and provisions, plus members of an unofficial St. Paul relief committee, Minneapolis representative J. T. Mannix, and pool reporters from the Twin Cities Press Association. The three-car special steamed north past station platforms crowded with solemn people. At a number of points, thoughtful individuals had hurriedly gathered items for the relief effort — not much, but enough to show their concern for the sufferers in the fire district. At White Bear people cheered when the Reverend Father R. T. Burke climbed on the train. He held the Victoria Cross, Great Britain's highest military honor, for heroic actions in Afghanistan. Few, however, noticed when Judge J. C. Nethaway boarded. He was determined to reach Hinckley.

The St. Paul relief train arrived in Rush City at 5:45 p.m., and promptly went to a side track. Railroad official L. S. Miller was on his way from Pine City with the special hospital train. While the train stopped for water, he briefed the St. Paul contingent, explaining that the Rink Hospital in Pine City temporarily served as the focal point of relief activities. He then sped down the line, continuing his errand of mercy. The St. Paul relief train rolled on to Pine City, unloaded, took on refugees, and started back south. A spectacular display of pyrotechnics from burning stands of trees lighted the way.[23]

George C. Dunlap, one of the Skunk Lake passengers fortunate enough to take the initial St. Paul relief train to the Twin Cities, had experienced a harrowing time. He and two others, Miss Scarvey and Mr. Hayden, had wandered away from Skunk Lake and waited out the fire in an open area. After the danger passed, they returned to the railroad, finding the tracks covered by a mass of iron work and other debris in place of the elegant coaches of the limited train. They met a Scandinavian who took them to two dugouts, where they spent a long and dreary night with about twelve other persons. "We were kept busy passing up the muddy water of a spring to many a thirsty survivor, who, as he drank, would falter out the story of his miraculous escape," Dunlap explained. On Sunday, when everyone returned to the wreck, they found only a few railroad workers. The handcars and No. 12 having already left, the refugees walked to Hinckley. There, they had to wait several hours for the relief shuttle, which took them to Pine City. At the Rink Hospital, they received treatment for their smoke-damaged eyes. Dunlap never forgot the trip from Skunk Lake to the Eastern Minnesota roundhouse. "The sights beheld that morning were horrible in the extreme," he said. "The dead bodies of men, women, children and cattle lay around in heaps on every side. I cannot dwell on the sickening spectacle."[24]

Yardmaster Dave Williams stayed in Duluth only long enough for railroad personnel to make up a combined construction and relief train. By 3:30 p.m., he had again started south. After he got off at the ruins of Finlayson, he took a party and started to scour the blackened countryside for rural survivors. Conductor Wellman proceeded south with the train, systematically repairing damage to tracks and culverts.

Two thoroughly organized rescue trains from Duluth left at 4:00 p.m. on Sunday, one heading out over the St. Paul & Duluth Railroad, the other on the Eastern Minnesota Railway. O. D. Kinney directed the former, designated the "Kinney." In addition to medical stores, the train carried six physicians, four trained nurses from St. Luke's Hospital, experienced woodsmen and "packers," and volunteer relief workers. Several well-known local politicians, including ex-Mayor C. D. Autremount of Duluth, had offered their services. There were also "Sordid Ghouls" who planned to loot the dead. A newspaper correspondent reported that three of the "infernal hounds" were discovered and thrown off the train.[25] The Kinney planned to penetrate as far as Miller, then send a party overland from there to Sandstone. The other train also hoped to send help to Sandstone. Under the direction of W. C. Farrington, general manager of the Eastern Minnesota, and J. N. Hill, it consisted of an engine, two flat cars, two freight cars, two day coaches, and a private car. The "Farrington" had a rescue staff of eight physicians and fifty woodsmen. Anticipating trouble with the terrain and the Kettle River, the railroad officials had included teams of horses, wagons, and even a row boat. One of the flat cars transported a large load of lumber: officials had decided they needed it for coffins.[26]

George B. Knight, one of the first relief workers from Rush City to reach Hinckley, had immediately begun to help victims and to cover the dead. In mid-afternoon on Sunday, as he ministered to the eyes of the "blinded and exhausted" train men from No. 45, one of them asked, "Has anybody gone to Pokegama?" Knight answered, "No, Why?" A shocked expression appeared on the railroader's face. He blurted out, "Our train was wrecked there. The people of Pokegama are in the cars, for God's sake go up!"[27] Through a horrendous error no one had gone to the wreck of No. 45. The crew had sat in the Hinckley yards for several hours, assuming that authorities had dispatched a relief expedition. The tired railroaders had even helped gather supplies. Now, they discovered that the people on the train remained unattended.

Knight and five other young Rush City men — W. S. Chapin, Edward Farrel, Gustaf Lingren, Robert O'Leary, and Frank Smith — mounted a handcar and pumped down the Eastern Minnesota in the direction of Pokegama. Advancing over the burnt and smouldering road proved a difficult task. Only a mile after starting, Smith decided he had made a mistake and wanted to go back. The others refused and pressed on. Smith sat and pouted, refusing to help pump. Three miles out of Hinckley the fire had burned a long trestle over a marsh. To continue their journey, the six men would have to carry the handcar a considerable distance through the slimy waters. A relatively easy task for section hands, it presented severe problems for amateurs. Lingren and Farrel joined Smith in objecting to going farther. After a bitter argument, the men reached a compromise. Lingren, Farrel, and Smith promised to wait with the handcar while the others, Chapin, Knight, and O'Leary, went ahead on foot, taking along a box of biscuits and a can of milk. After a two-mile walk, they arrived at the wreck. The three rescuers did what they could to relieve the suffering among the people, formed them up, and led them back to the handcar, each of the Rush City men carrying a child. When the column made the handcar, enterprising individuals enlarged it with rails and boards, enabling everyone to get aboard. All the Rush City men, now reunited in purpose and spirit, fell "manfully" to work. On the three-mile trip to Hinckley the push car had to be unloaded and lifted around culverts and defective rails no less than fifteen times. After the rescue effort came to a successful conclusion, the six men wanted to start out again, intending to go all the way to Pokegama. Officials of the Rush City Relief Corps, however, vetoed the plan: the men appeared tired and it was getting on toward dark. A fresh crew would attempt the trip on Monday.[28]

Late in the afternoon, a second relief unit from Mora reached the lath car. Dr. Cowan appeared first, riding on a contraption called a train velocipede, a light vehicle in which one rider provides all the power. Having brought bandages and liniments, he quickly ministered to the many people with eye trouble. Two handcars followed, carrying food and drink. "We can take some of you back with us," yelled one of the rescuers.[29] Everyone eagerly accepted the invitation, except for Dr. C. A. Kelsey, his family, and a few others — all determined to stay and start rebuilding. Although this may have sounded irrational under the circumstances — the embers had not yet cooled and the dead remained unburied — no one questioned their decision to remain. The rest started to Mora on the handcars. "So, surrounded by kind and sympathizing friends, this forlorn party went on to Mora, reaching there after dark," Lucy Kelsey wrote. "On the way, one of our friends jumped off the car and ran up the steep bank, bringing back with him the large bag of cranberries gathered by Mabel and Alice Nelson the afternoon of the fire, and left by them on the outskirts of the burned district. Though we had to get off while the men carried our hand cars around the burned ties and bridges, in places, we went on with lightened hearts to a friendly reception in the pleasant and hospitable town of Mora."[30]

At midnight, two men from the Kinney, who had walked the five miles from Miller Station, aroused the people at Hell's Gate. Misinterpreting their shouts, some refugees panicked. "Is there fire in this house also?" someone yelled.[31] It took a while to quiet the refugees down and to convince them that no danger existed. After they dressed, the people started through the pitch dark night to Miller, many wearing no shoes and some with hardly any clothes. "Arriving at the train, we were taken in hand by kind and sympathetic friends and refreshed with food and tender care," the Reverend Emil Anderson declared. "The doctors dressed our wounds, and experienced, tender nurses cared for our sick." Anderson felt grateful to both God and man for the timely relief from the "terrible devouring flames."[32]

Even while the medical workers tended those from Hell's

Gate, woodsmen from the Kinney chopped an overland trail to Sandstone. After they completed their task at about 2:00 a.m., they found 247 people, including the Friesendahls, and brought them back. The woodsmen, many of them huge men of tremendous strength, carried little children on "their great broad backs."[33] After everyone had boarded the Kinney, it reversed to Duluth, arriving at 7:25 Monday morning.

The other Duluth train, the Farrington, after an exasperating delay caused by an engine derailment in Duluth, finally reached the end of the usable roadbed at Partridge. There, the only things left unburned were the trucks of the boxcars. After burying Robert Burns, the only Partridge resident to die, and helping four refugees from the remote Nelson's lumber camp, the relief party divided into two groups.[34] One struck out overland toward the Sandstone quarries; the other thrust straight down the railroad. Each person carried a knapsack full of food, axes, shovels, and lumber. Smoke from burning roots and stumps filled the air, making breathing somewhat difficult. The two parties came together at the Kettle River, then worked down the steep bluffs to the north bank. For a short time they did not think they would get across; they had left the rowboat at the train. Just when someone had decided to go back for it, a man on the other side saw them, pulled over on a twelve-foot flat-bottom boat, and ferried the rescuers across. In the quarry office they found the "prostrate forms" of twenty-eight frightfully burned women and children, all alive; the physicians started at once to alleviate the suffering. After determining that all the other survivors had left, either for Hell's Gate or the Kinney, the relief directors made a grim decision. They knew that a necessary task remained in Sandstone, the one for which they had brought the wood.[35]

Chapter 8

"In Handling the Bodies We Made a Stretcher with Two Poles"

Monday, 3 September, was a busy day for the political and business leaders of Minnesota. No one expected any help from Washington, the federal government having no relief or disaster programs. In addition, President Grover Cleveland's response to the Panic of 1893 and the depression that followed indicated that he was not inclined to involve his administration in lavishing money on the victims of a forest fire in faraway northern Minnesota. For reasons of policy and philosophy, the President, a Democrat, refused to support relief programs for unemployed workers. Although Minnesota could expect private donations, it would have to take care of its own, against the backdrop of a national economic crisis that had shaken faith in the system.

Mayor William H. Eustis of Minneapolis had spent a busy Sunday night. He stayed at the newspaper office reading the grim headlines in the first edition of the Minneapolis *Tribune*: "A CYCLONE OF WIND AND FIRE! Northern Minnesota and Wisconsin Bathed in a Sea of Flame and Hundreds of Human Lives Are Sacrificed to the Insatiable Greed of the Red Demon As He Stalks Through the Pine Forests on His Mission of Death. TWO HUNDRED DEAD AT HINCKLEY. The Awful Story of the Destruction of the Town and the Appalling Loss of Life Graphically Told by Correspondents of the *Tribune*. Flames from the Surrounding Forest Sweep Down Upon the Village, and Being Caught by a Cyclone, Dance in Ghoulish Glee, Leaving Hundreds of Charred Corpses in Their Wake. BURNING OF THE DULUTH 'LIMITED.' While the Train is on Fire From One End to the Other the Passengers Make Their Escape Into a Marsh, and Lying Down in the Water, Save Their Lives. Ten or a Dozen, However, Jump From the Coaches Into the Sea of Roaring Flame and Are Burned to Death — Thrilling Story of a Mad Race With the Fiery Flames." Preliminary estimates placed the death toll at 355.

Early on Monday morning, Eustis convened a meeting of

the Citizens' Relief Committee of Minneapolis at the Commercial Club. It was a carefully orchestrated affair. On his motion, Charles A. Pillsbury, the most important man in Minneapolis and probably in the state of Minnesota, took the chair. President of the largest milling concern in the world, he was a millionaire many times over. After making brief remarks stressing the need for immediate action, Pillsbury called for opinions from the floor on the best way to proceed. A lengthy and tedious discussion followed. Although some people present came from other walks of life, the majority belonged to the Minneapolis Chamber of Commerce, the controversial manufacturing organization that controlled and monopolized the flour industry. They were the movers in Minneapolis. At an appropriate time, Pillsbury recognized one of the members, P. B. Winston, who introduced a resolution that naturally passed: "Whereas, Terrible and destructive forest fires have visited the Northern part of our state causing great loss of life, and rendering homeless hundreds of our fellow citizens. Resolved. That the chairman of this committee is authorized to appoint a committee of twenty-one, for the purpose of securing immediate relief for the sufferers, and that the committee is empowered to increase this committee and to appoint other committees with full power to act. Resolved, further, that the Mayor of this city is requested to call a special meeting of the city council tonight, to take such action as is in their power for the relief of the fire sufferers."[2] The resolution had the effect of circumventing the democratic process. Pillsbury named an executive committee, which, while including Mayor Eustis and a few religious leaders, consisted primarily of businessmen. Then, after accepting the donation of two army cots, thanking the Adams' Express for offering to carry provisions free of charge to the fire zone, authorizing the manager of the Bijou Theater to hold a benefit performance, and establishing a subcommittee to draw up a memorial for engineer James Root, the Citizens' Relief Committee adjourned.[3]

At 12:30 p.m. in St. Paul, the seven-member executive committee appointed by the General Relief Committee, a body created by Mayor Robert A. Smith, convened at the Chamber of Commerce building and did several things. It elected business leader E. W. Peet chairman, established a finance committee to solicit and manage cash contributions, and organized a supplies committee authorized to handle all nonmonetary gifts and to appoint appropriate subcommittees. The executive committee agreed to meet daily at noon over lunch at a private club.[4]

The Duluth Citizens' Central Relief Committee steadily expanded its activities, bringing together many voluntary services. While hotels and restaurants continued to provide food and quarters, several churches turned basements into temporary dormitories. The Pilgrim Congregational Church cared for ninety-eight children; the First Presbyterian Church became a combination hospital and housing unit; after renting the Berkelman Block, St. Paul's Episcopal Church turned it into a relief center. The Reverened C. C. Salter provided shelter for fire victims at the Bethel, the local rescue mission. The Odd Fellows donated their hall. St. Mary's Hospital, St. Luke's Hospital, and the Maternity Hospital coordinated disaster programs. The upper-class members of the Ladies' Relief Society started a clothing drive, with somewhat unexpected results.[5] An observer reported, "As soon as it became known that they . . . had established headquarters, contributions commenced to pour in, and continued to pour by single garments, by bundles, and by wagon loads, good, bad and indifferent (for the poor were vying with the rich) in a constant stream, until the poor gentlewomen having the place in charge were almost buried in the heaps of donations, and asphyxiated by the old-clothes-reek that prevailed."[6]

Pine City's relief efforts accelerated and increased in scope. James Hurley, chairman of the Pine City Relief Committee, expanded the membershp as more rescuers arrived, adding Judge J. C. Nethaway of Stillwater, Minneapolis representative J. T. Mannix, and others. As staff became available, Hurley established an executive committee and a number of subcommittees to bury the dead, distribute provisions, collect money, aid distressed women, manage supplies, and handle transportation. Hurley correctly perceived that he needed a large operation to cope with the many problems that had emerged since Pine City and its Rink Hospital had become a center of relief activities. The Reverend William Wilkinson, explaining the village's role, wrote, "To Pine City, telegrams came from near and far like a flood, one man could not possibly have done the work. Telegrams to persons who had relatives in the fire and from relatives to those who had escaped its heat and flames, from all sorts of people offering help and asking questions. Crowds flocked to Pine City on foot, in wagons and buggies, and by trains, the representatives of the state, of the great cities; lawyers, doctors, clergymen and nurses; every rank in society found this a convenient place. The refugees might be seen upon the streets, men upon whose faces the terrible anxiety of the fatal Saturday had stamped an indelible mark; they were too sad to speak; women who had little children in their arms, into whose faces they looked and took a sweet pleasure in so doing, even though they knew that to provide for these little ones meant for them years of dreary work, hard toil and sacrifice; children out of whose lives had departed the comforts of other years. Some of these people had escaped death only by most wonderful providence. There was one common bond of sympathy, and that was that they had all had similar, though different experiences."[7] Not all the persons who came into Pine City were there for legitimate reasons. On Wednesday, 5 September, a large number of toughs arrived, their "boisterousness" necessitating the closing of the saloons and the bringing in of police reinforcements.[8]

Rush City formalized its committee on Monday morning at a combined meeting of the council and citizens. The gathering appointed three men, F. S. Christensen, J. D. Markham, and R. H. Grant, to administer jointly the already-functioning Rush City Relief Corps. Furthermore, the council and the citizens approved a $250 gift to the Pine City Relief Committee and arranged daily carloads of milk to the fire victims at the Rink Hospital. Robert Nerrel, a farmer from near Rush City, generously donated sheep and cattle. The local Masonic lodge pledged $600.

Other Minnesota communities went ahead with relief measures. At St. Cloud, the city council, meeting at the early hour of 7:30 on Monday morning, set up a committee to purchase provisions and made arrangements to send physicians and trained nurses to Pokegama. When the city's relief train pulled out at 12:45 p.m., it carried two medical doctors and many politicians, including six aldermen, the city clerk, and the street commissioner. Mayor D. W. Bruckart, who stayed behind, ordered the police to distribute an appeal for aid, which stated: "There is much suffering, the result of forest fires that have lately swept over the country round Hinckley. We this day sent a car load of provisions to Brook Park (Pokegama). They need clothing and bedding. We will send teams to your doors at about 5 o'clock this afternoon to receive such contributions as you feel able to make. Have them ready."[9]

Mora's efforts were no less significant. Even though the hamlet initially had no formal relief mechanism, the town hall and the church became relief centers for the Pokegama survivors. People contributed bedding and clothing. After spending the night by the pool, John Gonyea received attention to his severe burns. On Monday morning, the village council appointed a three-man committee, appropriated $50, and sent a message to the mayor of St. Paul asking for help. Mankato, almost 150 miles from the seat of the fire, typified the response of other cities in the state. Fifty businessmen met at the Board of Trade in response to a public call. They established a committee to collect relief funds, ultimately raising $1,031.38 for the Hinckley victims.[10]

Governor Knute Nelson of Minnesota acted on early Monday afternoon. By then he had tested the political winds and ascertained the extent of the calamity. He had difficult problems. He wanted to avoid any personal blame and keep the powerful lumber interests from falling under attack, at the same time helping the stricken people. Except for performing such ceremonial duties as visiting hospitals and shaking hands with sufferers, he decided to stay in the background. After consultation with his aides, he appointed a five-man State Commission. As expected, it had a strong business composition: Charles A. Pillsbury, Charles Graves of Duluth, Matthew Norton of Winona, and Kenneth Clark and Hastings H. Hart of St. Paul. Pillsbury, already, of course, head of the Minneapolis relief effort, provided a necessary link with the Minneapolis Chamber of Commerce. Norton was a lumberman with a reputation for "prudent and honest business methods." Graves was former speaker of the Minnesota House of Representatives. Clark headed the Capital Bank of St. Paul. Hart, Chairman of the Minnesota Board of Corrections and Character, had the only nonbusiness credentials.[11] On the surface, Nelson's commission seemed to benefit his own political fortunes more than those of the unfortunates, but political realities needed serving.

Newspapers throughout the land carried extensive reports of the Hinckley fire. Yet a whole series of fires on 1 September

130

tended to mute the news. The huge temperature inversion spawned numerous blazes in the Upper Midwest. In north-western Wisconsin and the upper peninsula of Michigan, gigantic fires burned swaths as much as twenty miles long through the woodlands, though the destructive flames moved slowly enough so that few people died. About fifty miles southeast of Hinckley, Barronett, a Wisconsin lumber village of 500 people owned entirely by the Weyerhaeuser Corporation, burned to the ground. Eight miles away, fire swept Shell Lake about 5:00 p.m., fifty-three buildings worth $100,000 going up in smoke. Nearby towns — Brashaw, Granite Lake, and Comstock — all suffered fire damage. Farther away, flames threatened the Wisconsin communities of Cable and Prentice, and the Michigan cities of Ironwood and Houghton. On Lake Superior, grey smoke from 15 million feet of burning lumber on the Washburn docks made it difficult to see in Ashland, across Chequamegon Bay. To make matters worse, remote parts of far northern Minnesota and western Ontario erupted into flames. Forest fires raged all along the Rainy River in the boundary waters from Lake of the Woods to Lake Superior.[12]

The relief workers from the Farrington went about their unpleasant activities in Sandstone — burying the dead. It was a hot and humid day. Since the bodies lay exposed to the heat, the men decided it impractical to make coffins. After grave-diggers dug trenches two feet in depth, the relief workers laid in them sixty-one sets of remains, each carefully marked, assuming that the Pine County coroner would eventually make more formal funeral arrangements.[13]

On Monday morning, Judge J. C. Nethaway, now an official of the Pine City Relief Committee, decided to undertake a trip to Sandstone. After commandeering a handcar at Hinckley, he loaded it with 150 boxes of bread, a few cartons of canned meat, some coffee and tea, plus cups and other utensils. He planned to go north on the St. Paul & Duluth to Miller Station, then cross east to Sandstone on a logging railroad he had learned about. J. D. Markham of the Rush City Relief

Corps, a Minneapolis *Tribune* reporter, and three other men went along on the expedition. They experienced considerable difficulty reaching Skunk Lake, having to carry the handcar around burned bridges and culverts. The state of the countryside shocked the journalist, who noted that the few trees left standing were charred to the height of forty feet. The peculiar tint of the ground made it look like a mixture of brown sand and gunpowder. All the grass had burned to the roots. "In bleak and dreary stretches of country in what is now a great lonely land, was seen the body of a deer whose fleet feet had not been able to outrun the flames, or of a human being, who had been absolutely powerless against the grim destroyer," he commented.[14]

At Skunk Lake the party found yardmaster Dave Williams and a wrecker clearing the tracks. Learning that the Sandstone survivors had gone to Duluth and that no railroad ran from Miller to Sandstone, Nethaway and the others decided to look for bodies west of Skunk Lake. Three hundred yards from the right-of-way they found the remains of Otto Rowley from No. 4. Rowley's death came as a surprise. An experienced railroader, who was General Passenger and Freight Agent of the Duluth and Winnipeg Railroad, he had violated a common sense rule and dashed blindly into the smoke after the train stopped. The men continued on, discovering the blackened form of a woman near a destroyed cabin. They had no way of identifying her. Next, they came upon the house of John Robinson, near Skunk Lake on the edge of the woods. Peering into the cellar, they saw Robinson's body, along with those of his wife and three children. "All the clothing was burned from the bodies, but the victims had evidently been suffocated before the flames reached them," the reporter wrote. "The hands of the oldest daughter were upraised with palms together in an attitude of prayer."[15] That spectacle proved enough for the reporter, Markham, and one of the rescuers. They went back to Hinckley. Nethaway and two others tramped on toward Grindstone Lake, planning to spend the night. Along the way they found dead squirrels, rabbits, pheasants, deer, and other wild game.

There were other people in that woods that Monday. Mr. and Mrs. Alex Cameron of Hinckley had gone fishing on

Saturday at Grindstone Lake. About 4:00 p.m., when the sky darkened, they lit lamps, but soon found the fire upon them. Running to their boat, they rowed toward the center of the lake, fighting heavy waves. Although they feared drowning, they considered it better than burning to death. The wind blew them all the way across the lake, where they found an abandoned Indian camp and cooked some potatoes. They remained there on Sunday, waiting for the ground to cool. The next day, they walked ten miles to Hinckley. Upon arrival, they were shocked to find the town destroyed and all of their belongings lost.[16]

The Reverend Emil Anderson had arrived in Duluth on the Kinney early Monday morning. After a hearty breakfast at the Armory, he felt fit enough to catch a 10:30 a.m. work train headed down the Eastern Minnesota to the temporary railhead at Partridge. In early afternoon the train pulled up behind the Farrington. Anderson and a party of gravediggers walked overland, arriving about 2:00 p.m. in Sandstone, in time to help the men already on the scene. They found whole families scattered about in wild confusion upon a field of death and horror.

Anderson helped check neighboring farms. At one place only one out of six family members lived through the fire. A potato field yielded thirteen bodies. The man who operated the waterworks floated face down in ten feet of water, having died at his post. A well which emitted a horrible odor held eighteen bodies, almost all small children. Another well contained a dead woman, unmarked by the flames, who appeared to be sitting and praying on a floating mattress. "Only a little ways from here, on a farm, we found a whole family in the cellar, standing together, with arms clasped around each other, leaning against the wall — all dead," Anderson declared. "While a neighbor, in a similar place, saved himself and family by having a great supply of milk on hand whereby the greedy flames were quenched."[17]

As the burial parties completed their unpleasant duties, a work train arrived from Hinckley, carrying Eastern Minnesota president Samuel Hill. He had gone south to Hinckley in mid-afternoon, after Dave Williams cleared the tracks at Skunk Lake and completed necessary repairs, getting the St. Paul &

Duluth back into operation over its entire length. Hill, of course, had a greater problem, the reason he had gone to Sandstone: he wanted to examine the Kettle River bridge. At Sandstone, after feeding a "little fellow," he walked up the line. Then, deciding he would need several hundred workers to make repairs, he returned to his train and went back to Hinckley. From there he issued a statement to the United Press: "The scene of death and ruin along the road is a terrible one. Not a sign of life is anywhere to be seen. All is a blackened, charred mass of ruins. Dead animals and human beings are everywhere, and they are burned wherever found. In one old well were found twenty-five snakes and forty or fifty field mice, all in together alive. There are many peculiar features of the fire. In one place, where all else was burned and blackened, we found a wagon with hay in the box intact, while the horses were dead."[18] The Reverend Anderson and some others who took Hill's train to Hinckley helped bury more bodies, until they boarded a 9:00 p.m. Duluth & St. Paul northbound train. Hill went on to St. Paul to meet James J. Hill, hurrying east from Helena.

After closing the last graves at Sandstone, the tired crews, including James Norman Hill, had gone back to the quarry office and transported twenty-eight injured people across the Kettle River and onto the relief trains, waiting at Partridge. The Farrington and the one that had come down Monday both reversed within minutes of each other at 7:00 p.m. and moved slowly back to Duluth-Superior, a sad trip, punctuated by the mournful sound of whistles. Rescuers and rescued had only the most unpleasant of memories.[19]

The relief train from St. Cloud could only get as far as Mora. By then, it had already dispensed most of its supplies. A forest fire had burned twenty-five homes at the important junction of Milaca, twenty-eight miles northeast of St. Cloud. Although no one died, many had lost their homes and downed wires had cut the town off from the outside world. In Mora, the St. Cloud politicians became embroiled in an argument with their counterparts from Mora. At first the Mora leaders refused aid, claiming they had the situation under control, but finally, the leaders worked out a compromise. The train unloaded its supplies and left a small party, including a physician and two nurses. The St. Cloud politicians and their train went back home, taking with them the injured John Gonyea and thirty-two Russian Jews who had no intention of ever returning to Pokegama. It was a strange ending to the first relief effort launched from St. Cloud.[20]

☆　☆　☆

On Monday evening, J. D. Markham, not only a relief official, but a partner in the firm that owned most of Pokegama, started toward there by handcar from Hinckley, accompanied by nine men. They came from different parts of Minnesota, many well known in their communities and in state affairs. Among those on board were Albert Berg, the Republican candidate for Secretary of State in the fall general election, and the Reverend William Wilkinson, the rector of St. Andrew's Church in Minneapolis and the former chaplain of the Minnesota House of Representatives. They had along two army tents, thirty pairs of blankets, food, axes, shovels, a fence post, and two lanterns. As they pumped off, a state senator and several physicians wished them well.

The going proved slow. "As the darkness gathered, far as the eye could reach, the blazing stumps of pine lighted up the distant scene, and gave to it an air of peculiar beauty," Wilkinson wrote. "But we were not on the lookout for grand scenes, or picturesqueness. All felt the sadness of the hour, and the importance of our mission."[21] They had to carry the hand-car around fifteen burned culverts and bridges, the worst passage coming at the marsh site that had stopped the young Rush City men from pumping farther the previous day. The marsh had become a large and burning peat bog. To get through, the Markham party had to shovel a path two to three feet deep and wide enough for the handcar. They reached the lath car at 1:00 a.m. Tuesday, finding Dr. C. A. Kelsey and the others adequately provisioned and in good spirits. With nothing to do, Wilkinson and the others distributed the blankets, said prayers, and went to sleep.[22]

☆　☆　☆

At 3:00 on the morning of Tuesday, 4 September, another relief train left Duluth for Partridge on the Eastern Minnesota

Railway, the "Bailey Expedition," its leader William T. Bailey, an experienced woodsman. He had with him thirty skilled lumberjacks and three clergymen. They intended to explore thoroughly the countryside around Sandstone for survivors and to bury the dead. After reaching the end of the track at 6:00 a.m., the jacks fanned out through the blackened woods. As peat bogs burned in many places, root systems continued to flare up, dead forest creatures lay about, and the woods lacked the familiar sounds of wind rustling through pine tops, birds singing, and beasts howling. At Sandstone, a few miserable farmers, huddled in what had been a shed, had come in from the country after the other relief parties had left. The scene was one of total desolation. Houses, buildings, barns, stables, and even fences had all burned, as had all crops except potatoes, saved by the sandy soil.

The Bailey Expedition found it difficult to penetrate the remote areas. Often, men's boots broke through the surface to the burning roots. In places, a foot or more of ashes covered the ground. One party, searching for the body of fourteen-year-old Flora Bilado, found her charred remains about 400 feet from where her mother and sisters had survived the conflagration. Flora, while her mother watched helplessly, had died engulfed in a sheet of flame fifty feet high. The woodsmen speedily constructed a box, dug a grave, and laid her away, as one of the clergy said a few words. Everyone then moved on to investigate other farms.

Late in the afternoon men checking a root cellar on the Peter Englund farm prodded the surface, uncovering part of a body. Because the place still smouldered and emitted intense heat, they decided to put off further examination until the following morning. When digging started on Wednesday, the results turned the stomachs of the most callous of the lumberjacks. Eighteen men, women, and children had jammed into a space six feet by six feet. Now all were dismembered, the heat had roasted their flesh, and only three of the bodies had heads. The jacks sorted out the victims as best they could, putting them in coffins which they carried to the cemetery and placed in a common grave. After a brief funeral service, they went back to work. In all, the Bailey Expedition interred twenty-three victims. They failed to find numerous people reported as missing — the fire had incinerated them.[23]

Some weeks later, a writer talked to Bailey at the Spalding

Hotel in Duluth. The woodman, asked for photographs of his group, said, "We did only what any men would have done, if they had been in our places. We never expected fame, and we do not want our names mentioned in the matter." When pressed about whether he actually helped remove eighteen bodies from the root cellar, he looked solemn, thought a minute, and replied, "Yes; it was only our duty."[24]

The Reverend William Wilkinson, who stayed in Pokegama to help find and bury the dead, received assistance from the remaining settlers, some St. Paul relief workers, and a divinity student. As an unexpected side duty, they had to haul huge piles of charred pine in order to cremate more than twenty-nine dead cows, oxen, and horses. In the course of several days, the workers found twenty-three sets of human remains, all without clothing and badly disfigured, many hard to identify. Although several were sent away for burial, most went to rest in temporary or permanent graves at Pokegama. Wilkinson particularly remembered presiding at the funeral of Jakey Braman, found a short distance from two dead horses, several hundred yards from the mill pond that saved many of the inhabitants. Wilkinson said the interment took place after willing hands had dug the grave on a bright and sunny day. "The burial scene was one to captivate the mind of an artist, who desires to portray love and service, life and death in their very best forms," Wilkinson recalled. So, Jakey, a Jew, received a Christian burial, a cross made out of a lath serving as a headmarker.[25]

Frank Webber directed the burial of the dead at Hinckley. Continuing hot weather necessitated that he complete the work as soon as possible, because he decided not to embalm any of the bodies. A Duluth *Evening Herald* correspondent, after seeing the piles of bodies, reported, "some burned to a crisp, others only browned by heat, and more with a fragment of clothing larger than a man's hand to conceal their awful nakedness."[26] Almost all the bodies, including the 125 in the swale north of town, were severely burned, and the swamp contained scorched and stinking flesh. There was danger of an epidemic. Webber, who had brought 5,000 feet of lumber for caskets from Pine City, had a crew of four professional undertakers, twenty-one volunteer gravediggers, and members of the Minnesota National Guard. The unidentified went into common graves. Webber became enthusiastic in explaining the methods he developed: "In handling the bodies we made a stretcher with two poles, and the bodies were rolled into the stretcher and from that into the trench, which was dug on an incline."[27] The slant made it easy to roll the bodies down to their final resting place, Webber reporting that he and his assistants handled 233 bodies in less than three days. He noted that although many of those engaged in the operation felt a need for "stimulants," he drank only a small amount of milk. He took pride in his contribution to the relief effort.[28]

A reporter for the United Press found the whole business pretty awful. Standing by the railroad, he saw two-score boxes, filled with bloated and disfigured forms, bearing such inscriptions as, "Supposed remains of Mrs. Blanchard, horribly distorted," and "Girl, ten years old, no clothing." As the journalist copied down the information, a man commented, "If you want to see a pitiful sight, go to the cemetery." The reporter started in that direction, picking his way through deserted streets full of dead horses, cows, chickens, cats, and dogs. Reaching his destination, he found half a dozen men digging a trench. Nearby, he saw "naked bodies — men, women and children — scorched, blackened, distorted, bowels and brains protruding, hands clutched in their final agonies, hair singed from heads, old, young, middle-aged, male, and female, all in a promiscuous heap."[29] In another part of the field he saw people poking through a pile of bodies five feet high. Mayor Lee Webster looked unsuccessfully for his wife.

The reporter saw many other horrible sights. Throughout town he viewed portions of human bodies: a hand, a leg, or a torso. He watched as workers placed what had been a child and an adult's leg into a coffin with a blackened man with exposed intestines. Some of the living disinterred graves, seeking loved ones. The shallow trenches in the cemetery emitted an awful stench. He wrote, "It is difficult to portray the situation at Hinckley. A few refugees, a half score of searchers, a team or two transporting boxes containing dead bodies, the places where a town had been — that is the picture. The brick veneer, which constituted the outer covering of some of the buildings,

138

has fallen into the cellars. It is like looking over the track of a cyclone. A few curious relic hunters delve among the ruined household goods, but their quest receives little reward."[30]

A journalist representing the Duluth *News Tribune* thought the earth "swept bare" and the soil "calcinated." The dead bodies reminded him of a poem:[31]

>The world is full of farewells to the dying
>and mournings for the dead.
>The voice of Rachel for her children crying
>will not be comforted.

The odor from the putrefying flesh of thousands of unburied dead animals polluted the Hinckley atmosphere, even as the last human victims were laid to rest, making things unpleasant for relief workers and for other persons. Many journalists, including photographers and artists from *Harper's, Frank Leslie's,* and other national publications, arrived. As if from nowhere, hundreds of sightseers appeared; police rounded up a "number of suspicious characters" and told them to "walk out" of town. Amidst the ruins, some Hinckleyites had already started to rebuild homes and businesses.[32] "Temporary buildings are being erected, lumber arriving this morning, and in a month Hinckley in her new dress will make her bow to the public," Angus Hay of the *Enterprise* wrote in a dispatch datelined 4 September. "Citizens are working with a vim and energy characteristic of the Hinckley people. They are bearing up well under their loss. The village will be grander and larger than ever, though the loss of some of her most prominent businessmen will be deeply felt."[33] Disasters seldom deterred nineteenth-century town promoters; they could always find the silver lining.

Searchers, led by Gustave Wenz and several timber cruisers, continued to roam the countryside. Almost all the bodies found needed an "unknown" classification — a lumberman about age thirty wearing a blue mackinaw and heavy boots, a girl estimated about sixteen years old, and the bones identified as those of a child of around twelve.[34] In some places, workers found piles of the distinctive grey ash left by cremated human bodies, sometimes using rakes in an attempt to determine if one or more persons had perished at the particular spot. Usually, they could only make an estimate. One group of bodies remained unburied, despite a confirmed report that the remains of twenty-three Chippewas lay scattered along ten miles of trail. Chief Wacouta and his entire band had perished. The gravediggers' decision not to cross the difficult country meant the Chippewas would be left where they fell, winter food for wolves and bears.[35] Considerable effort, on the other hand, went into trying to find the bodies of two Hinckley fishermen, J. T. Clark and Tom Campbell, last seen on the way to Lake Eleven. A search party taking spades along, intending to bury the men on the spot, suddenly saw two men coming toward them, carrying fishing gear. It was Clark and Campbell, alive and well. After the fire passed, they had continued their angling expedition. They did not understand why those who ran toward them shouting greetings had shovels rather than fishing rods until told the reason.[36]

The combined religious organizations of Pine, Mille Lacs, and Carlton counties scheduled a gigantic memorial service for Sunday, 9 September, at Robinson's Park in Pine City. What followed one newspaper called a "Day of Terror."[37] Fires continued to burn in the vicinity, an erroneous report that a sheet of flames, 200 feet high, was about to strike Pine City holding down attendance and forcing a temporary postponement until the reports proved false. By then dusk had arrived and a light rain fell. Officials moved the event indoors to Tierney's Hall. One of those present declared, "The scene at the hall was a heartstirring one. There were those present who alone represented what remained of a once happy family. Some were still bandaged; upon others frightful scars were visible, and the look on the faces of many told only too plainly the story of the loss of home, loved ones and hope. Sadness pervaded the atmosphere and a heavy feeling seemed to press on the hearts of all present."[38]

As expected, the ceremonies were long and tedious. J. T. Mannix, the Minneapolis official who coordinated that city's relief trains, acted as chairman. After the Reverend Peter Knudsen of Hinckley read the Scriptures, Bishop Mahlon N. Gilbert followed with a prayer and a woman sang an anthem. Knudsen then stepped forward to read a list of those in his congregation who perished. Commenting on the havoc caused by the flames, he claimed the hand of God was behind the cloud of sorrow. Next came the reading of a memorial poem,[39] followed by "words of courage and comfort to the sorrowing" and a sermon by Father Bajec, "Is Life Worth Living?" The cleric concluded that it was. "When I looked upon the cold, distorted corpses as they lay scattered upon the blackened ground and thought of how suddenly fire had taken them from life; how they had struggled for a foothold upon plenty amidst hardships and discouragements, and how family ties had been rent asunder and grief was all there was left, it certainly seemed that life was not worth living," he intoned. "But, my friends, there is hope beyond, and those persons who are now cold in death were slowly preparing for an eternal home."[40] When Father Bajec finished, J. D. Markham gave an account of the expedition he led to Pokegama and advised worshippers that his company still had plenty of cheap land for sale near the community. When he finished his sales pitch, Albert Berg, back campaigning for the position of Minnesota Secretary of State, sang two solos. A supporter recorded, "His rich, powerful, wonderful voice was indeed music to the ears of those who had heard nought but sobs and distress during the week."[41]

At long last, Bishop Gilbert gave the main address. He praised Pine City — "this little community, before obscure and scarcely discovered" — for aiding the victims of "God's whirlwind." He claimed the Civil War and the Hinckley fire both were part of a divine plan to bring freedom to the United States, because the finger of God "swept away all distinction of rank and class." He told how hardened St. Paul businessmen had cried after hearing of the suffering of poor and obscure people in the flaming pineries, the human calamity touching their hearts. He believed that "God thus used the grim surgery of fire to heal the wound" between rich and poor in Minnesota. Next, he talked about how plain men — Powers, Best, Sullivan, Root, and Blair — had provided lessons of "divine" valour. Bishop Gilbert sermonized, "Such heroism will cover a multitude of sins, and I doubt not God will blot out some of their faults, for they doubtless had faults, and remember that they nobly did their duty in the time of trial. The trial seems hard but what matter if it makes you better? Look up and let the sacrifice of friends and loved ones make you nobler and purer. Last of all, when the grass has grown green over their graves and your hearts' wounds are somewhat healed, let us not forget that God came down in a chariot of fire one day as he did for Elijah of old to take our better selves up to himself."[42] The services concluded with the processional hymn, "Out Great Redeemer Praise Ye." Seven days that started with politicians and businessmen ended with clerics.

Chapter 9
"Heroism and Bravery"

Disasters appear suddenly out of the blue, receive major notice, and then seemingly vanish as quickly as they came. They do not lend themselves to analytical discussion. The Hinckley fire ran the normal course. After receiving national headlines for a week, it receded from view. The press associations withdrew their reporters and the Minnesota papers went back to publishing other matters of concern on their front pages, downgrading articles about the fire sufferers to the inside sections. Yet the disaster needed a final accounting. The relief agencies had to wrap up their activities, the politicians had to study the blaze in the light of possible legislation, the experts had to produce suitable explanations, the heroes needed rewarding, and the communities and communication systems required rebuilding.

Of the many relief agencies that dealt with the tragedy, the State Commission established by Governor Knute Nelson ranked as the most important in terms of prestige, effort, and money. The Commission worked quickly and submitted a report on 31 December 1894.[1] It cooperated with local relief agencies, telegraph companies, railroads, and business groups. The Commission received large quantities of unsolicited secondhand clothing and other items, in addition to five full carloads of flour, which came from an anonymous donor. The various donations, ranging from flour from Grand Forks to shoes from Montgomery Ward & Co., had a cash value of $10,700. Cash receipts totalled $113,476.84 and disbursements $104,843.95. Although most of the cash came from sources in Minnesota, some $14,711.19 arrived from other parts of the country and $11,600 from overseas. Lord Mount Stephen of England and Sir Donald Smith of Canada, both involved with Hill and his railroad interests, each gave $5,000, Lady Smith contributing $1,000. The two largest amounts subscribed inside the United States were New York Life's $1,000 and the New York Stock Exchange's $1,100.[2]

The Commission members regarded themselves as agents of the donors in extending aid. They ruled out trying to make good financial losses suffered in the fire. "We have considered it a matter of chief importance to render such assistance as should restore these people to a condition of self-support and relieve them as speedily as possible from a dependent condition; and it gives us much pleasure to report that in most cases the relief given has been instrumental in accomplishing this result, and that a large majority of the people who have been assisted are now in a position of self-support," the report stated.[3] In keeping with this philosophy, the Commission tried to hold down salaries for relief workers. "Outsiders" made $17,814.69 and "paid sufferers" $7,970.29. Administrators received a little more than $6,000; the rest went mostly for carpenters and laborers.[4]

The builders made an effort to hold down costs by constructing standard 16' x 24' houses, boarded and covered with drop siding. Furniture allotments were made on a sliding scale, starting with a formula based on the needs of a family of five. Sufferers determined to have lived in shacks prior to the fire received between $40 and $100 in building materials. A few young men were given larger amounts of lumber than otherwise by promising to marry their girl friends. In the final accounting, the Commission aided 2,636 of a reported 3,181 survivors.[5]

The people of Duluth believed that their relief committee and the organizations under its umbrella made a major contribution. Working for over three months, chairman E. C. Gridley of the Citizens' Central Relief Committee functioned out of a large room in the building housing the Duluth *Evening Herald*. Various subcommittees had tables on either side of the room, printed cards on the walls identifying their functions. Gridley, a good organizer, quickly brought order out of "a state of general chaos." His operation reminded many of a well-run bank. Volunteers toiled every day for six weeks, frequently for long hours and into the night, most giving their time at the neglect of their own business interests. "No one can imagine unless one went through it what a tax on ones nervous strength that was," two executive committee members wrote. "Not once was Mr. Gridley unequal to any emergency which arose, and with the utmost courtesy and kindness treated all who came under his immediate care, answering and deciding in the same spirit all the difficult questions, and deciding with great promptness, and clear and fair-mindedness, all the varied problems which arose constantly before him."[6]

Gridley, with the full backing of Mayor Ray Lewis, demonstrated his control of the situation when Governor Knute Nelson and two members of the State Commission, Hart and Charles A. Pillsbury, came to Duluth on 6 September for a Thursday evening meeting at the Spalding Hotel. Gridley refused to let the distinguished visitors intimidate him. If they had hoped to take away jurisdiction, they went away disappointed. At the end of a two-hour meeting, they agreed that Duluth would continue to handle temporary relief for all refugees inside the city until they could provide for themselves or the state had the resources to deal with their plight. The state officials visited relief centers, including the Armory and Berkelman Block.[7] They gave words of encouragement and promised assistance. Pillsbury said, "The farmers will be sent back to their farms. . . . The men and heads of families must be disposed of as quickly as possible."[8] Then, Pillsbury, Nelson, and Hart went back to the railroad station, there taking a train for St. Paul. Gridley and Lewis saw them off.

Duluth agencies cared for over 1,500 refugees, the vast majority of Norwegian and Swedish extraction. "I found the refugees to be rather above the average in intelligence and moral tone, well behaved and sympathetic," an observer noted. "Saw no one intoxicated during their stay at the Bethel." At the height of relief activities, the committee fed over 1,000 persons daily, and housed almost as many. The hospitals cared for thirty-four people, among them the horribly burned Peter Bilado of Sandstone and the exhausted Father Lawler of Hinckley. The Maternity Hospital reported three children born to fire sufferers, one set of happy parents naming their child James Paul Duluth Crocker. Many touching scenes made the $40,000 effort worthwhile. One occurred when the Reverend C. C. Salter of the Bethel joined together in matrimony Minnie Samuelson and John de Rosier. Scheduled to be married the day of the fire, each thought the other died in the flames. Reunited, they went through with the ceremony. Chief of Police H. T. Armstrong of Duluth escorted the bride who wore a light-colored dress given her by the Ladies' Relief Society. A reception followed.[9] Thus, life slowly returned to normal.

Other cities continued their relief programs for several weeks. The St. Cloud committee aided dozens of people in the Pokegama and Milaca area, where flames had destroyed many country homes. The organization raised close to $1,000, almost half by sponsoring a sightseeing tour to Hinckley.[10] The citizens of Mora, an extremely self-reliant group, spent a great deal of time helping the people in Pokegama. Suspicious of outside help, the Moraites actually turned down outside subscriptions of money, including one $25 gift from R. C. Dunn of Princeton, Minnesota.[11] The executive committee of the General Relief Committee of St. Paul, which continued to meet until 12 November 1894, collected $25,098.28, plus a special $5,000 contribution from James J. Hill. Relief trains and other supplies cost $12,054.01, the rest of the money ultimately going to the State Commission.[12] In Minneapolis, Charles A. Pillsbury's Citizens' Relief Committee spent close to $30,000 before completing its work on 22 October 1894. The following spring, 2,500 people attended a concert given by the Minneapolis Musicians' Association in Exposition Hall that raised $1,200 for fire sufferers. Mayor William H. Eustis gave a speech in which he told of the deeds of heroism and self-sacrifice that occurred during the fire. At Rush City, peak relief efforts occurred in the first days after the disaster. Heavily loaded trains moved in and out of the station, many spending lengthy stays. Then, within just a couple of days, things returned to normal.[13] Much the same happened at Pine City. The Rink Hospital reverted to its former function as a skating rink and the citizens returned to their usual activities. The committee in Pine City received many donations. In his final report of 12 January 1895, James Hurley reported receipts of $2,599.21 and disbursements of the same amount.[14]

Those singled out for heroic services received appropriate recognition. A group of Hinckley residents honored engineer

Edward Barry and conductor W. D. Campbell of the freight train with solid-gold medals in the form of six-pointed stars suitable for watch charms, the inscription telling of their "heroism and bravery."[15] James Root of No. 4 received a resolution from the citizens of Minneapolis, signed by the mayor. Part of the tribute stated, "The loftiest impulse which animates the human breast is that which prompts one to self-sacrifice for the salvation of others. . . . The merit of his heroic deed attaches not alone to him, but also to the craft of which he is a member. The lives of thousands upon thousands of people are hourly in the hands of locomotive engineers, and seldom has one proved false to his trust, or failed to rise to the emergencies which confronted him. Such an emergency which tried the mettle of manhood confronted James Root on this occasion, and he proved himself its master. Two hundred human beings today owe to him their lives. On that Saturday morning he was a locomotive engineer; today he is a hero."[16]

On 12 September the black leaders of St. Paul held a "well-attended meeting" at Market Hall to honor porter John W. Blair of No. 4, several white passengers, either in person or by letter, attesting to Blair's exemplary conduct and leadership ability. C. D. O'Brien gave a speech in which he said Blair had done his duty, "typical" of the black race, and told how the brave porter performed on the train and at Skunk Lake. "For three-quarters of an hour we stood in a flame that is as indescribable as the flames of hell," O'Brien emphasized. "John Blair might have left the party and sought his own safety, but he was too much of a man for that. He stood there, a willing sacrifice, until the last passenger was safe. It was not the bravery of a trained soldier or a sailor, but that of a poor porter of a chair car, keeping his mind to follow out the dictates of a heart as pure and as noble as any that ever beat in a human breast. It is well to honor such men and teach our children to emulate their example. I am proud to be alive to take him by the hand and thank him for his humanity." With that, O'Brien left the podium, walked to where Blair sat, and vigorously shook his hand, displaying deep feeling.

Other tributes followed. The Reverend R. C. Quarles, black minister of the Pilgrim Baptist Church, claimed the "blazing headlines" had slighted Blair. "I am glad, John W. Blair," Rev. Quarles said, "that among those who had the coolness and manhood to make a record on that terrible night, that there

was a black face with a white heart." F. L. McGhee, the only
black attorney in St. Paul, presented Blair with a badge engraved on one side with a picture of the burning train and said
that blacks always did their duty. He continued, "We can not
fittingly honor him as it is fitting he should be honored. But
when called to appear before the judgment seat, John W. Blair,
then and only then will you receive your full reward. I have
here a little token of recognition of your heroism. It is from the
people of that race from which you spring. Wear it. It is but
a poor monument to the memory your conduct merits as com-
pared with the honor that conduct has been to us." Next,
railroad officials gave Blair a solid-gold watch engraved:
"Presented by the St. Paul & Duluth R. R. Co. TO JOHN
WESLEY BLAIR for gallant and faithful discharge of duty on
Limited train, No. 4, in Forest Fires, Sept. 1, 1894." Finally,
Blair spoke, doing so with dignity: "All I can say is that on that
awful night I did what I thought to be my duty. The memories
of this night and the kindness you have shown me shall always
be cherished by me as long as I live." Then he sat down.[17]

Of all the major participants in the affair, only conductor
Thomas Sullivan came close to censure. His leaving the scene
of the wreck upset many people, who thought it conduct un-
called for in a railroad official of his rank. They refused to
believe that a black porter could possibly have had the situation under control. On top of that, Sullivan did not help things
by eventually breaking down and requiring many days of hos-
pitalization. In a state of confusion he made disordered comments about tossing a child out of a window of his train. No
such incident happened, but the early newspaper reports carried
it as a fact. The Duluth *Evening Herald*, after stating that
Sullivan was "crazed and was unable to talk," immediately
quoted him as shouting, "I threw the child out the window.
Is she saved?" The *News Tribune* said that Sullivan was "out
of his mind."[18] Then, too, Superintendent Robert Bell claimed
he found Sullivan sitting on a bench at Miller Station, moan-
ing, "O, Mr. Bell, all the passengers are burned!" Bell claimed
he took charge from that point onward.[19] Slowly, things
straightened out. Passengers had nothing but praise for Sullivan's
conduct. R. S. Farrell, who observed Sullivan at the Miller

148

Station, reported no indication of "derangement." William
Blades said, "Conductor Sullivan was in his right mind, or appeared to be, as long as I saw him."[20] The newspapers and press
associations corrected initial reports, giving Sullivan the credit
he deserved. As for Sullivan, he said in a statement issued from
his hospital bed, "I will say in conclusion that any one man
deserves no more credit than another, as none of us did any more
than our duty which we owe to our employers and to the public
in our charge."[21]

☆   ☆   ☆

Many poets wrote about the fire. Some were in a sad vein,
as the following by Elton T. Brown:[22]

Gone from the haunts, where they loved and
    they lingered,
Gone from the paths that their feet loved to roam,
Bereft are the friends that revered and that mingled
Daily with those whom the fire has called home.

Men stricken down in the bloom of their manhood,
Women, whose hearts were proven true as steel.
Children, whose eyes had brought life to the
    household,
Suffered and died, still mute with appeal.

These were heroes, whose story will ne'er be
    related,
These were heroines too, who will e'er be unsung,
Self-sacrifice truly, of all attributes noble,
Thy name from the top of the peak should be flung.

They are gone, leaving naught but the ashes
    behind them,
They are gone, yet we can but rejoice at their gain,
Their trials are all over, no ill can betide them;
While we must work on, till we meet them again.

Horace Wilcox authored a ballad more specific in terms of factual information, which appeared on 14 September 1894 in the
Pine County Pioneer, entitled, "The Hinckley Fire." He used

the same meter as "The Night Before Christmas":

> The fire swept o'er us with terrible wrath
> And left desolation and terror strewed in its path,
> The flames approached with a sickening crash
> And fair Hinckley town disappeared like a flash.
>
> But Hinckley saw another sight
> As the afternoon grew dark as night,
> When, like the handwriting on the wall,
> The population recognized Jehovah's call.
>
> Fly for your lives; come let us fly,
> That we may escape the fire that descends from
>   the sky.
> The elements of destruction more fiercely blew,
> While amidst heartrending scenes the death
>   list grew.
>
> Oh! what a sight for mortal eyes,
> To witness the sight of a mother's agonizing cries!
> With a babe clasped protectingly on her breast,
> Hurrying through the elements to join the
>   unfortunate unrest.
>
> On through the flames the refugees fly,
> Some find shelter and more lay down to die.
> Down by the river they pause for breath,
> But are instantly swept to a terrible death.
>
> The southbound Limited ran their train to
>   Skunk Lake shore,
> Through fire and smoke and an awful roar,
> While fathers and mothers were praying amid
>   the din,
> The brave engineer was successfully battling their
>   lives to win.
>
> Jim Root is a man who knows no fear,
> God bless the iron nerve of this brave engineer,

With his hands all blistered and his clothes
    all aflame
This hero of heroes pulled through just the same.

Among the heroines who ran with great zeal,
Was a certain young lady, Miss Mollie McNeal,
    [sic., Molly McNeil]
She ran half fainting up the railroad track,
This brave young girl had no chance to look back.

The Eastern Minnesota Train Number Four,
Pulled into Hinckley just before the roar;
When all at once the fire spread over them with
    a darkening hue,
And for that train the stricken ones fairly flew.

They crowded that train some four hundred
    or more,
Some were bleeding and some were frightfully
    sore.
"God in heaven, save us," they despairingly
    cried,
Then the brave engineer, regardless of orders,
    started back on his perilous ride.

The bridge at Kettle was all afire, when some
    cried, "Pull the pin
We will leave the train here and save ourselves,
    we can run safely in."
But the brave engineer with indignation cries:
"Whoever touches that connection instantly dies."

This brave and tender-hearted engineer's name
    is Best,
And he said, "If I have to die, I shall go with
    the rest."
This man deserves a golden chest.
And when he departs for another world, there he
    will mingle with the best.

Franklyn W. Lee tried to immortalize "Jim Root's Ride," in a
verse patterned after "Casey at the Bat":[23]

When the angel blows his trumpet and the
    firmament unrolls,
And the voice of God is calling all the many
    scattered souls,
There's a man who'll lead a phalanx up the
    jeweled golden street
To a corner they have saved for him beside the
    mercy seat;
For the angels hate a coward and they love
    a gritty man
And they know Jim Root's a hero on the strictly
    gritty plan.

It was early in September, and the earth was
    just as dry
As a lump of punk and hotter than an upper
    Congo sky.
There had been no rain since April and it
    needed but a match
To engulf the northern district, set it burning
    like a thatch;
And the people did not wonder when the smoke
    began to rise
Till a pall hung low and darkly, shutting out
    the summer skies.

Jim was running on the Limited, and when he
    left Duluth
There were stories of the dangers which seemed
    only partial truth,
But the hand that held the throttle was a hardy
    one and true,
And though hell was on his orders, Jim was
    bound to take her through.
He controlled the lives of many and he knew
    that all his nerve
Would be needed when he headed for the hades
    round the curve.

They had made the run to Miller ere the breeze
    began to scorch

Ere the people saw the waving of that mighty,
    flaming torch;
"But I'll run her through to Hinckley," thought
    the little engineer,
"Where I'll wire for orders — it is not too far
    from here";
And he yelled to Jack McGowan, who was on
    the other side,
"Crowd the coal and keep her going, for I mean
    to let her slide!"

All the horrors told by Dante, all the pictures
    by Doré
Are imperfectly suggestive of that blazing
    right of way,
For the universe seemed flaming and the air
    would fairly seethe
Till the people in the coaches found it difficult
    to breathe,
While the entrance into Hinckley seemed the inner
    gate of hell,
With the devil's imps disporting on the pine
    trees as they fell.

To have passed beyond the station would have
    meant the death of all;
To have fooled around for orders from some
    fellow in St. Paul
Would have been the height of folly, and when
    people who had ran
For the train were safely sheltered from the
    fiend the flight began,
And, reversing, Jim moved backward through the
    awful, blazing rain
To a place where he could harbor all the people
    on the train.

There were flames above, around them,
    underneath — no hand could paint
All the terrors of that moment, which made
    strong men droop and faint.

Every car was like an oven; coaches blistered
    in the heat;
Panes of glass began to shrivel, and, to make
    the hour complete,
Tongues of flames crept through the windows
    as the train began to burn
And a strange and deathlike whiteness crept
    o'er faces drawn and stern.

But Jim Root was on the engine and had naught
    to bar the flame,
Though his hand was on the throttle and he
    stuck there just the same,
As he backed her through the horror, with Skunk
    Lake six miles away,
He had little hope of living to recall that
    fearful day;
But the engineer was plucky, and with Jack
    McGowan there
He was good for any duty, for he had a life
    to spare.

When his hand began to blister, why, the other
    was strong,
And when both were singed and broiling they
    did duty right along;
When his overalls were smoking, there was
    hardy, faithful Jack,
Who was standing with a bucket pouring water
    down his back.
Once or twice Jim almost fainted, once or twice
    fell off his seat,
But he rallied like a hero as he fought away
    the heat.

And he saved the train of people, just for
    common duty's sake —
Held the throttle, cool and gritty, till they
    reached the little lake,
Till the hundreds went in safety from the
    charred ill-fated train,
And he never gave a whimper in his agony of pain,

Never murmured — no, not even when his
  fearless ride was o'er
And he sank, all burned and nerveless, on the
  blackened, burning floor.

They will tell you of the heroes who left no good
  deed undone;
They will say that all the honor should not go
  to merely one;
But whatever men accomplish for the grateful
  ones to tell,
When in future years they speak of all the
  horrors of that hell,
It was Jim, who, sticking bravely in the glaring
  face of death,
Saved three hundred human beings from the all
  destroying breath.

When the day of judgment cometh and the
  firmament unrolls,
And the voice of God is calling all the many
  scattered souls,
There's a man who'll load a phalanx up the
  jeweled, golden street,
To a corner they have saved for him beside
  the mercy seat;
For the angels hate a coward, and they love
  a gritty man,
And they know that Jim's a hero on the
  strictly gritty plan.

The transportation and communication companies worked
hard to get their systems back into complete operation, the
Western Union Telegraph Company and the North American
Telegraph Company quickly repairing lines. The restoration of
normal traffic helped both relief work and railroad construction. The telegraph concerns placed their facilities at the disposal
of the State Commission, without charge or limit. Then, too,
they allowed the railroad section foreman to tap the wires at
any point, accelerating the logistics of track laying. Men, equip-

ment, and material could be sent quickly to crucial locations. Both railroads had major tasks. The St. Paul & Duluth, in addition to rebuilding stations and section houses, had to make major repairs to twenty miles of track, replacing 22,000 ties and long stretches of warped or otherwise damaged rails. The Eastern Minnesota needed to re-lay twenty miles of track between Pokegama and Partridge. The biggest task involved the rebuilding of the Kettle River bridge. Timber had to be cut on short notice near Duluth and transported to the river. Within days, over 300 men toiled at the site, James J. Hill personally supervising some of the construction work. Framing started on 7 September and at midnight on 16 September the first train rolled across. The bridge was out of commission only fifteen days. John Finlayson, the master carpenter on the project, felt that a "very good record" for reconstructing a span 850 feet long and 132 feet high. Once the railroads opened, they continued to help the relief effort in numerous ways. They offered free transportation for fire victims and their relatives, in addition to hauling materials and provisions at no cost. Although this was humanitarian, it was also very practical. The lines had an economic stake in recovery — they needed the traffic and they owned two million acres of land in northern Minnesota.[24]

The Hinckley Fire caused an estimated $12,000,000 in damage and officially killed 413 of the estimated 3,500 people in the region on 1 September 1894. Some 270 died at Hinckley, 80 at Sandstone, 25 at Pokegama, 15 at Miller, and 1 at Partridge,[25] many others perishing in remote parts of Pine County. Hundreds received injuries. A United Press reporter was wrong when he wrote, "It appears that it was a clean-cut case of either life or death. Most of those who escaped did so without any physical hurt, while those who were unable to do so perished."[26] Actually, the Red Demon had made it impossible to determine the exact toll. Many bodies were dismembered. Relief workers buried countless others in common graves. Flames burned people to ashes. So, what became the official count actually amounted to only a rough figure. More than 600 may have died.[27]

Rebuilding went ahead rapidly at Hinckley. Lumber companies brought in crews to frame buildings, preparing for thousands of lumberjacks needed for a great crash logging program. To prevent serious storm damage, all the standing pine trunks in the burned district needed harvesting over the winter months. One concern soon had 1,200 jacks working within eight miles of Hinckley, cutting and banking 150 million feet of logs. A single gigantic load hauled at a camp north of Hinckley contained fifty-six logs, scaled at 37,120 feet.[28] For a short time, Hinckley became again a busy lumber camp. "All is alive with activity," Lucy Kelsey gushed after a 27 October 1894 visit. "New dwellings are springing up as by magic, while larger business blocks are taking shape."[29] Reconstruction went ahead with no apparent plan, the new Hinckley as ugly and nondescript as the old — a collection of one- and two-story frame houses and clapboard buildings. As before, most of the structures were built south of the Grindstone River in between the railroads. Survivors reclaimed their own property and proceeded accordingly. A significant change took place, however, that only a long-time resident would have noticed. Except on the main street, the residents set the structures farther apart than before. Of course, Hinckley had already seen its greatest day when the fire hit, and after the lumber companies finished the massive cutting programs, it had no need for as many buildings. The town dropped in population, becoming just another small Minnesota country village. It even lost the county seat to Pine City.

The other places affected by the fire experienced varying fortunes. Miller and Finlayson, which had never had more than a few houses clustered around small stations, soon rebuilt. So did Partridge. Within a short period, life returned to normal, centered around the sawmill. Mission Creek was barely a town when the fire began. With the mill moved away, it would have lost any real reason for being. After the conflagration, a few people returned and built houses, but the majority left for other parts. They had no attachment for the place; it was just another camp. Despite the brave statements of the Kelsey-Markham Land Co., Pokegama never succeeded. While a hard core of settlers doggedly tried to build a viable community, most left and few new ones arrived. Sandstone, however, had a far different situation. The quarries soon employed over 150 men, producing stone for the railroads, the Eastern Minnesota making the town a division point.[30] Reconstructed before the first snow, Sandstone soon approached Hinckley in population and became a more stable economic unit. Some observers, forgetting the cost in human lives, felt the fire actually helped advance Sandstone's limited fortunes.

Strange events connected with the fire perplexed people. So strongly blew the wind that the survivors heard trees crashing in the nearby woods half an hour or more before the fire swept through. Some of the men, women, and children who jumped into wells either suffocated or were broiled alive; others who did the same thing survived with a minimum of discomfort. Many who sought safety in open areas or in water made it through, while just as many who did the same thing lost their lives. Near Hinckley, a farmer lay in a field until the air cooled, arising to find everything within twelve feet of where he stood burned to a crisp. Almost everyone in the fire district reported "tongues" and "sheets" of fire. The very air seemed to burst into flame and the heavens rained burning cinders. Trees that appeared whole at first glance had burned-out trunks. In some places, only stumps remained; there were no trunks still standing. A young sapling grew in good condition six feet away from a tree thirty inches in diameter that burned from the roots upward. A large haystack lay unscathed in a blackened meadow; a tar-paper shack was entirely untouched, while all the trees around it burned. In a pigpen, the heat roasted one hog to death, while its companion escaped relatively uninjured. A claim shanty covered with ragged tar paper remained standing, while green timber piled alongside went up in smoke. No one could tell what the Red Demon would do as he went about the grim work of destruction.[31]

Many speculated about the cause of the massive conflagration. Some refused to accept the explanation that the blaze resulted from a combination of prolonged drought, unusual climatic conditions, and the cutting practices of the timber companies. Numerous divines saw the hand of God behind the flames: the Almighty wanted to try the settlers in Pine County by fire, either to punish them for their sins or to break down economic differences. John Stone, the Pine City man who first flashed the news of the fire to the St. Paul newspapers, placed the blame entirely on "Dame Nature." He said, "The fire at

Hinckley was one of the results of causes which are constantly
increasing in power and frequency, and which will, in the near
or distant future, develop much more disastrous effects. This
fire resulted in the constituent elements of the air becoming
disintegrated, separated, and leaving one element — an inflammable, dangerously explosive gas, while the other hung like a
dark pall over the scene, shutting out the light and rendering
the chance for destruction more weird and complete. Literally
the air was on fire, exploding in flashes."[32] The insurance companies that faced heavy losses in the fire district presented a
different theory. In a formal proceeding, they charged that
unidentified "timber thieves" started the fire by igniting their
cuttings in order to cover their tracks.[33] That kind of sophistry
convinced nobody. Swedish-born Minneapolis journalist Gudmund Akermark stated bluntly: "Was it human beings who in
wickedness or in order to cover their crimes, brought this about?
We *can* not and *will* not believe it."[34]

The 1895 Minnesota State Legislature impaneled a Pine
Land Investigating Committee to make an inquiry and recom-
mend possible legislation. In early April the committee made
an inspection trip to the fire district, the representatives, mainly
farmers dressed in their Sunday best, touring the zone. They
posed for photographers in Hinckley, at the Kettle River, and
around Skunk Lake. After returning to St. Paul, they concluded
their work and supported the successful passage of Minnesota's
first comprehensive forestry law. The leading feature of the
measure made all town supervisors fire-wardens, adopting a
system successfully used throughout New England. Because of
parliamentary maneuvering by supporters of the timber industry
and laissez-faire economics, the legislation did not create a forest
commission. Instead, it made the Minnesota State Auditor the
Fire-commissioner, authorizing him to appoint a deputy, called
the Chief Fire-warden, to execute the act. A first draft of the
bill gave the Chief Fire-warden only police duties. However,
legislator W. P. Allen of Cloquet led a fight that successfully
added a provision requiring the official to "investigate the extent of the forests in the state, together with the amounts and
varieties of the wood and timber growing therein, the method
used if any to promote the re-growth of timber, and any other

important facts relating to forest interests which may be required by the Forest commissioner. The information so gathered, with his suggestions relative thereto, to be included in a report to be made by him annually to the Forest commissioner." This gave the Fire-warden scientific and research responsibilities.

By prearrangement, the State Auditor appointed Christopher C. Andrews the Fire-warden, his prophetic and insightful comments about how to prevent forest fires, published right after the Hinckley disaster, making him the logical choice. At age sixty-five, Andrews accepted the challenge, even though he knew it was only a start. He initially had a salary of $1,200, an authorized budget of $6,000, and an emergency fund of $5,000 reserved for spending only during dry and dangerous seasons. Andrews estimated that the forests of Minnesota had a value of at least $100 million. "They were scattered over about seven hundred organized townships and a large unorganized territory — altogether about twenty million acres," he wrote. "In a country where thousands of new settlers were struggling to clear their land, and were sorely tempted in dry weather to burn their brush and rubbish; in a wilderness frequented by land seekers and mineral prospectors, hunters, and tourists, all of whom were likely to have camp fires; in a region containing hundreds of logging camps and traversed by two thousand miles of railroads, including logging-roads; one can well imagine the liability of fires. It takes many men to keep close surveillance over twenty million acres of forest land." Andrews performed his duties for the next sixteen years. At times he had to exert political pressure to prevent the legislature from abolishing the office. He could not even get a bill requiring logging companies to remove slashings out of committee. Only the gradual awareness of a second generation of loggers that conservation helped business and a series of other disasters — Chisholm in 1908, Baudette in 1910, and Moose Lake in 1918 — brought a well-coordinated system of forest rangers and a fairly adequate budget. "Work to prevent fire is but one part of forestry," Andrews said at the end of his tenure. "One of my duties was to bring the cause of forestry in all its phases before the public." The single positive aspect of the Hinckley Fire was that it enabled him to gain an official means of accomplishing his purpose.[35]

Persons who had their lives affected by the Hinckley disaster gradually resumed normal living. The relief workers went back to their old jobs. Some cut trees for low salaries; others operated great corporations. A few bragged about their contributions; most preferred to remain in the background. To their credit, none of the politicians involved in helping victims, with the possible exceptions of Governor Knute Nelson and candidate-soloist Albert Berg, exploited their contributions for personal advantage. Railroaders, from the Hill family on down to the humble brakemen on No. 24 combination train, went back to operating their trains, convinced they had saved hundreds of lives and miffed at accusations that they had no business running passengers into the fire district on the afternoon of 1 September 1894. Engineer James Root summed matters up when he observed that Minnesota always had forest fires during the summer months; everyone took them for granted.[36] After a short convalescence at his White Bear home, he again sat at the throttle of crack St. Paul & Duluth passengers. On some runs, conductor Thomas Sullivan, fully recovered, punched tickets back in the coaches.

At Pokegama, Dr. C. A. Kelsey struggled to recoup lost funds in land ventures. Alexander Berg erected a new store, Mrs. Carver reopened a boarding house, and Hans Nelson resumed duties as station agent. The Batys, Bramans, Frances, and Frames returned to farming. Lucy Kelsey, with her husband and children, went back to their former home, where she wrote a book about her experiences, *The September Holocaust*. In Sandstone, the Lifebrers, who survived, stayed, as did the Bilados, who lost two daughters. M. W. W. Jesmer continued to work as a bridge guard for the Eastern Minnesota. Peter Peterson, the quarry superintendent, found himself running a much larger crew. Pat Regan returned to shift work at the quarry. The Friesendahls rebuilt their home within forty days. Emil Anderson, in keeping with earlier plans, matriculated in divinity school. Farmer Lars Mattis, who jumped down a well, marveled at his escape, when he learned that the neighboring Brods all died in the flames. Mrs. Garrity's establishment returned to business by the middle of December. Molly McNeil, the young girl who escaped from Hinckley on No. 4 and spent the night at Skunk Lake in company with a large coiled snake, returned to Hinckley and the surviving members of her family. Fire Chief John Craig reorganized the volunteers; Mayor Webster, shaken by the loss of his wife, attempted to pick up the scattered pieces of his career. The Reverend Peter Knudsen and Father Lawler resumed their ministries. Dr. Stephan again practiced medicine in Hinckley. Angus Hay resumed publication of the Hinckley *Enterprise*. "When we again hear the song of birds in the summer," he stated, "and the golden grain is being gathered in autumn from the fertile soil around Hinckley, the tale of the great Hinckley fire will be still being told."[37]

A silent spring did not come to the blackened pineries in 1895. New growth began with the first warm weather. By the end of summer a green undergrowth covered the forest floor, shooting up between the rocks, stumps, and small pine trunks unprofitable to market. Columbines and blueberries flourished where before they would never have had the required sun. Although the forest primeval no longer existed, animals returned, as did the birds. For the time being, corporations and settlers no longer interfered with nature. But things would never be the same again. Nine decades later, after almost all the participants were gone, scars remained. The area looked like cutover, a legacy of Hinckley's contribution to the industrial revolution in America.

Appendix

Important Trains and Handcars

SATURDAY, 1 SEPTEMBER 1894

Engine 19, St. Paul & Duluth (Duluth to St. Paul)
    Engineer C. P. Fadden
    Fireman N. Reider
Accommodation Train No. 45, Eastern Minnesota (St. Cloud
    to Hinckley and return)
    Engineer William Vogel
    Fireman Joseph Lancher
    Conductor Edward E. Parr
    Express Messenger John Sanderluis
Freight Train No. 23 down and No. 24 up, E. M. (West Superior
    to Hinckley and return)
    Engineer Edward Barry
    Fireman A. R. Thistle
    Conductor W. D. Campbell
    Brakeman C. C. Freeman
Passenger Train No. 4, E. M. (Duluth to Minneapolis)
    Engineer William Best
    Fireman George Ford
    Conductor H. D. Powers
    News Agent George S. Cole
    Judge Seagrave Smith
Passenger Train No. 4, St. P. & D. (Duluth to St. Paul)
    Engineer James Root
    Fireman John McGowan
    Conductor Thomas Sullivan
    Porter John Blair
    Superintendent Robert Bell
    L. S. Meeker
    C. D. O'Brien
    George C. Dunlap
    State Senator Frank Daugherty
"Way-freight" No. 12, St. P. & D. (at Willow River)
    Engineer Peter Kelly

Conductor John Roper

7:05 p.m. "Short Line" Relief Train, St. P. & D. (Duluth to Willow River and return)

Yardmaster David H. Williams

General Agent C. M. Vance

Freight No. 22, E. M. (at Dedham)

Engineer George Van Pelt

Conductor J. C. Cardle

Rush City Work Train, St. P. & D. (Rush City to Hinckley)

Engineer John Jones

Conductor Jim Sargent

Section Foreman John Powell

Handcar, St. P. & D. (Hinckley to Mission Creek)

Angus Hay

Carl Veenhoneen

Handcar, St. P. & D. (Mission Creek to Hinckley)

Section Foreman John Powell

Handcar, St. P. & D. (Miller Station to Skunk Lake)

Superintendent Robert Bell

Conductor John Roper

Yardmaster David H. Williams

Special Section of Passenger Train No. 3, St. P. & D. (Pine City to Hinckley)

Conductor Buckley

Conductor Jim Sargent

Dr. E. E. Barnum

Pine City relief official James Hurley

Handcar, St. P. & D. (Hinckley to Skunk Lake)

Section Foreman John Powell

Conductor Buckley

Conductor Jim Sargent

Dr. E. E. Barnum

Angus Hay

"Advanced Guard," St. P. & D. (Rush City to Pine City)

Dr. J. E. Gemmel

Dr. A. J. Stowe

Attorney and speculator J. D. Markham

Rush City Relief Train, St. P. & D. (Rush City to Pine City)

Dr. Krogstadt

Dr. Tietin

Handcars, St. P. & D. (Pine City to Hinckley)
  Physicians
  Rush City relief officials
St. Cloud Work Train (St. Cloud east and return)

SUNDAY, 2 SEPTEMBER 1894

Special, St. P. & D. (St. Paul to Rush City)
  Assistant General Manager L. S. Miller
"Silk Stocking" Relief Train, St. P. & D. (Duluth to Rutledge
  and return)
  President J. L. Greatsinger of Duluth and Iron Railway
  President Samuel Hill of the Eastern Minnesota
Work Train, E. M. (West Superior to Partridge and return)
  J. N. Hill
  Superintendent M. V. S. Thome
  Road Master Deviny
Passenger Train No. 1, St. P. & D. (St. Paul to White Bear,
  where stopped)
  Judge J. C. Nethaway
Handcar, E. M. (Mora to Pokegama)
  Section Foreman Ole Nelson
Work Trains, E. M. (St. Cloud east to repair bridges and return)
St. Paul Relief Train, St. P. & D. (St. Paul to Rush City)
  Minneapolis representative J. T. Mannix
  Judge J. C. Nethaway
Hospital Train, St. P. & D. (Pine City to St. Paul)
  Assistant General Manager L. S. Miller
Combined Construction and Relief Train, St. P. & D. (Duluth
  to Skunk Lake)
  Yardmaster David H. Williams
"Kinney," St. P. & D. (Duluth to Miller Station)
  O. D. Kinney
"Farrington," E. M. (Duluth to Partridge)
  General Manager W. C. Farrington
  J. N. Hill
Handcar, E. M. (Hinckley toward No. 45)
  George B. Knight

"Velocipede" and Handcars, E. M. (Mora to lath cars and Pokegama and return)
Dr. Cowan

MONDAY, 3 SEPTEMBER 1894

Handcar, St. P. & D. (Hinckley to Skunk Lake)
Judge J. C. Nethaway
Lawyer and speculator J. D. Markham
Work Train, E. M. (Duluth to Partridge)
Rev. Emil Anderson
Work Train, E. M. (Hinckley to Sandstone and return)
President Samuel Hill
Relief Train, E. M. (St. Cloud to Milaca)
Handcar, E. M. (Hinckley to Pokegama)
Lawyer and speculator J. D. Markham
Candidate Albert Berg
Rev. William Wilkinson

TUESDAY, 4 SEPTEMBER 1894

"Bailey Expedition," E. M. (Duluth to Partridge)
Woodsman William T. Bailey

Footnotes

CHAPTER 1: "The Red Demon of the North"

[1] Agnes M. Larson, *History of the White Pine Industry in Minnesota* (Minneapolis, 1949), 153, 238.

[2] Robert W. Wells, *Fire at Peshtigo* (Englewood Cliffs, N.J., 1968), 202-213.

[3] New York *Times*, 9 October 1871. There are dozens of accounts of the Chicago fire. The information used in this study is from a comprehensive academic history of the city, Bessie Louise Pierce, *A History of Chicago*, 3 vols. (New York, 1957), 3:3-19.

[4] Sir Howard Douglas-Bart is quoted in Rev. William Wilkinson, *Memorials of the Minnesota Forest Fires in the Year 1894 with a Chapter on the Forest Fires in Wisconsin in the Same Year* (Minneapolis, 1895), 12-14, which contains a good summary of the tragedy.

[5] Wells, *Fire at Peshtigo*, is the definitive work on the conflagration. The Associated Press reported the fires raging throughout the Upper Midwest and Ontario to the nation. For example, see the New York *Times*, 9, 10, 11 October 1871.

[6] Wilkinson, *Memorials*, 15-16; Gudmund Emanuel Akermark, *Eld-cyklonen eller Hinckley-branden*, William Johnson, trans. (1894; Askov, Minn., 1976), 114-115.

[7] Quoted in Alice E. Andrews, ed., *Christopher C. Andrews: Pioneer in Forestry Conservation in the United States: for Sixty Years a Dominant Influence in the Public Affairs of Minnesota: Lawyer: Editor: Diplomat: General in the Civil War, Recollections: 1829-1922* (Cleveland, 1928), 291.

[8] William Watts Folwell, *A History of Minnesota*, 4 vols. (St. Paul, 1930), 4:386-388; Theodore C. Blegen, *Building Minnesota* (Boston, 1938), 382.

[9] Quoted in Wilkinson, *Memorials*, 17.

[10] *Ibid.*, 17-19.

[11] Elton T. Brown, *A History of the Great Minnesota Forest Fires: Sandstone, Mission Creek, Hinckley, Pokegama, and Skunk Lake* (St. Paul, 1894). 5-6, 227-228.

[12] *Compendium of the Eleventh Census: 1890*, pt. 2 (Washington, 1894), 643, 786, 866; *Report on the Statistics of Churches in the United States at the Eleventh Census: 1890, vol. 9*, (Washington, 1895), 68.

[13]*Report on the Statistics of Agriculture in the United States at the Eleventh Census: 1890*, vol. 5 (Washington, 1896), 214-215, 334, 372, 438, 477.

[14]*Report on Manufacturing Industries in the United States at the Eleventh Census: 1890*, vol. 6, pt. 1 (Washington, 1895), 480-481.

[15]The St. Paul & Duluth Railroad schedule is from Brown, *Great Minnesota Forest Fires*, 30-31; the Eastern Minnesota Railroad schedule is from Wilkinson, *Memorials*, 132.

[16]Brown, *Great Minnesota Forest Fires*, 10-11; *1890 St. Paul & Duluth Time Table*, on display in the Hinckley Fire Museum.

[17]Edward W. Durant, "Lumbering and Steamboating on the St. Croix," in *Collections of the Minnesota Historical Society*, vol. 10, pt. 2 (St. Paul, 1905), 654; Brown, *Great Minnesota Forest Fires*, 10.

[18]*The Hinckley Enterprise: Commemorated to the Survivors of the Great Hinckley Fire* (Hinckley, n.d.). This is a publication of the Hinckley Fire Museum. Brown, *Great Minnesota Forest Fires*, 29-30; Wilkinson, *Memorials*, 44-47.

[19]Lucy N. A. Kelsey, *The September Holocaust: A Record of the Great Forest Fire of 1894* (Minneapolis, 1894), 7-15.

[20]Wilkinson, *Memorials*, 27.

[21]Kelsey, *September Holocaust*, 16-27.

[22]Quoted in Wilkinson, *Memorials*, 37.

[23]*Ibid.*, 83.

[24]Sanderluis is quoted in *Ibid.*, 266; Brown, *Great Minnesota Forest Fires*, 212.

[25]Brown, *Great Minnesota Forest Fires*, 215.

[26]*Ibid.*, 24; Frank R. Holmes, *Minnesota in Three Centuries*, 4 vols. (n. p., 1908), 4:225; Akermark, *Hinckley-branden*, 84.

[27]Brown, *Great Minnesota Forest Fires*, 22-23.

CHAPTER 2: "Escape for Your Lives. Hinckley Will Be Destroyed!"

[1]Stewart H. Holbrook, *Burning an Empire: The Story of American Forest Fires* (New York, 1943), 14; Duluth *Evening Herald*, 6 September 1894.

[2]Quoted in Rev. William Wilkinson, *Memorials of the Minnesota Forest Fires in the Year 1894 with a Chapter on the Forest Fires in Wisconsin in the Same Year* (Minneapolis, 1895), 60.

[3]Quoted in *Ibid.*, 63.

[4]Quoted in Elton T. Brown, *A History of the Great Minnesota Forest Fires* (St. Paul, 1894), 71.

[5]Wilkinson, *Memorials*, 21-23.

[6]Quoted in *Ibid.*, 37.

[7]Lucy N. A. Kelsey, *The September Holocaust: A Record of the Great Forest Fire of 1894* (Minneapolis, 1894), 61-64.

[8]Brown, *Great Minnesota Forest Fires*, 67-69.

[9]Wilkinson, *Memorials*, 32.

[10]*Ibid.*, 41.

[11]*Ibid.*, 42-43.

[12]*Ibid.*, 42.

[13]*The Hinckley Enterprise* (Hinckley, n.d.).

[14]Wilkinson, *Memorials*, 33, 41-42; Kelsey, *September Holocaust*, 91, 104.

[15]Kelsey, *September Holocaust*, 66-69.

[16]Quoted in Wilkinson, *Memorials*, 266-269. Sanderluis is called "Vandersluis" in Brown, *Great Minnesota Forest Fires*, 192.

[17]Quoted in Wilkinson, *Memorials*, 23.

[18]Quoted in *Ibid.*, 61-63.

[19]Quoted in *Ibid.*, 51.

[20]Quoted in Brown, *Great Minnesota Forest Fires*, 165.

[21]*Ibid.*, 212.

[22]Quoted in Wilkinson, *Memorials*, 181-183.

[23]Quoted in *Ibid.*, 179.

[24]Quoted in *Ibid.*, 165.

[25]*Ibid.*, 74.

[26]Cole is quoted on page 176 and Best on page 167 in *Ibid.*

[27]Quoted in Gudmund Emanuel Akermark, *Eld-cyklonen eller Hinckley-branden*, William Johnson, trans. (1894; Askov, Minn., 1976), 12.

[28]Quoted in Wilkinson, *Memorials*, 51-52.

[29]Quoted in Brown, *Great Minnesota Forest Fires*, 200.

[30]Quoted in Wilkinson, *Memorials*, 173.

[31]Quoted in Brown, *Great Minnesota Forest Fires*, 206.

[32]*Ibid.*, 57-60.

[33]Quoted in Wilkinson, *Memorials*, 157-158.

[34]Quoted in *Ibid.*, 167.

[35]*Ibid.*, 61-68.

[36]Quoted in *Ibid.*, 63.

[37]Brown, *Great Minnesota Forest Fires*, 165, 172-174, 178-179.

[38]Quoted in *Ibid.*, 171-172.

[39]*Ibid.*, 174-176.

[40]Quoted in Wilkinson, *Memorials*, 169; Brown, *Great Minnesota Forest Fires*, 209.

[41]Quoted in Brown, *Great Minnesota Forest Fires*, 166. The same account appears in *The Hinckley Enterprise*.

[42]Quoted in Wilkinson, *Memorials*, 169-170.

[43]Quoted in Brown, *Great Minnesota Forest Fires*, 200-202.

[44]*Ibid.*, 60, 211-212; Wilkinson, *Memorials*, 63.

[45]Akermark, *Hinckley-branden*, 33-34; Brown, *Great Minnesota Forest Fires*, 55-56, 211.

[46]Quoted in Wilkinson, *Memorials*, 63-64.

[47]Quoted in *Ibid.*, 181-182.

[48]Brown, *Great Minnesota Forest Fires*, 207; Akermark, *Hinckley-branden*, 99; *Hinckley Enterprise*.

[49]Brown, *Great Minnesota Forest Fires*, 212.

[50]Both quotes by Fraser are in *Ibid.*, 181-183.

CHAPTER 3: "For God's Sake Will You Save Us?"

[1]Elton T. Brown, *A History of the Great Minnesota Forest Fires* (St. Paul, 1894), 139.

[2]*Ibid.*, 147-149.

[3]Meeker is quoted in the Minneapolis *Tribune*, 3 September 1894; Gorman in Gudmund Emanuel Akermark, *Eld-cyklonen eller Hinckley-branden*, William Johnson, trans. (1894; Askov, Minn., 1976), 52; O'Brien in Brown, *Great Minnesota Forest Fires*, 154; Dunlap in Rev. William Wilkinson, *Memorials of the Minnesota Forest Fires in the Year 1894 with a Chapter on the Forest Fires in Wisconsin in the Same Year* (Minneapolis, 1895), 152-153.

[4]Root is quoted in Brown, *Great Minnesota Forest Fires*, 140. The quotes attributed to the elderly women and Bartlett are in his account. See also Wilkinson, *Memorials*, 129.

[5]Quoted in Wilkinson, *Memorials*, 129.

[6]Quoted in *Ibid.*, 147-148.

[7]Quoted in Brown, *Great Minnesota Forest Fires*, 155-156.

[8]Minneapolis *Tribune*, 3 September 1894.

[9]Quoted in Wilkinson, *Memorials*, 142-143.

[10]Quoted in *Ibid.*, 129-131. See also Brown, *Great Minnesota Forest Fires*, 141.

[11]Quoted in Duluth *Evening Herald*, 7 September 1894. See

also Wilkinson, *Memorials*, 163; Brown, *Great Minnesota Forest Fires*, 158.

[12]Blades and Daugherty are quoted in Wilkinson, *Memorials*, 139, 145; Gorman in Akermark, *Hinckley-branden*, 52.

[13]Quoted in Minneapolis *Tribune*, 3 September 1894.

[14]Quoted in Wilkinson, *Memorials*, 149.

[15]Quoted in *Ibid.*, 131-132, and in Brown, *Great Minnesota Forest Fires*, 143.

[16]Quoted in Wilkinson, *Memorials*, 143-145.

[17]Quoted in *Ibid.*, 131.

[18]Duluth *Evening Herald*, 7 September 1894.

[19]Quoted in Minneapolis *Tribune*, 3 September 1894.

[20]Quoted in Wilkinson, *Memorials*, 154.

[21]Quoted in *Ibid.*, 145.

[22]Quoted in *Ibid.*, 141.

[23]Brown, *Great Minnesota Forest Fires*, 50; *The Hinckley Enterprise: Commemorated to the Survivors of the Great Hinckley Fire* (Hinckley, n.d.).

[24]Quoted in Minneapolis *Tribune*, 3 September 1894.

[25]Brown, *Great Minnesota Forest Fires*, 180.

[26]Quoted in *Ibid.*, 157-159.

[27]Wilkinson, *Memorials*, 149-180; Duluth *Evening Herald*, 7 September 1894.

[28]Quoted in Wilkinson, *Memorials*, 150.

[29]Minneapolis *Tribune*, 3 September 1894.

CHAPTER 4: "Make for the River"

[1]Quoted in Rev. William Wilkinson, *Memorials of the Minnesota Forest Fires in the Year 1894 with a Chapter on the Forest Fires in Wisconsin in the Same Year* (Minneapolis, 1895), 170-171, 179.

[2]Quoted in *Ibid.*, 158.

[3]Elton T. Brown, *A History of the Great Minnesota Forest Fires* (St. Paul, 1894), 37; Gudmund Emanuel Akermark, *Eldcyklonen eller Hinckley-branden*, William Johnson, trans. (1894; Askov, Minn., 1976), 62-63.

[4]Quoted in Wilkinson, *Memorials*, 176, 182.

[5]*Ibid.*, 74.

[6]Quoted in Brown, *Great Minnesota Forest Fires*, 38.

[7]Quoted in Wilkinson, *Memorials*, 74-75.

[8]*Ibid.*, 185; Brown, *Great Minnesota Forest Fires*, 38-39.

[9]Quoted in Akermark, *Hinckley-branden*, 75.

[10]Stewart H. Holbrook, *Burning an Empire: The Story of American Forest Fires* (New York, 1943), 18-19.

[11]Brown, *Great Minnesota Forest Fires*, 65.

[12]Quoted in Wilkinson, *Memorials*, 83-84.

[13]*Ibid.*, 78-79.

[14]*Ibid.*, 79-81.

[15]*Ibid.*, 86-89.

[16]Akermark, *Hinckley-branden*, 64.

[17]Duluth *News Tribune*, 29 August 1976. Alex Friesendahl, who lived in Duluth in 1976, also survived the Moose Lake forest fire of 1918.

[18]Quoted in Wilkinson, *Memorials*, 75-78.

[19]Quoted in Brown, *Great Minnesota Forest Fires*, 186-190; Akermark, *Hinckley-branden*, 80-83; Wilkinson, *Memorials*, 108.

[20]Quoted in Akermark, *Hinckley-branden*, 75-76.

[21]Quoted in Wilkinson, *Memorials*, 89-91.

[22]*Ibid.*, 91.

CHAPTER 5: "The Country Is All Burning Up"

[1]Rev. William Wilkinson, *Memorials of the Minnesota Forest Fires in the Year 1894 with a Chapter on the Forest Fires in Wisconsin in the Same Year* (Minneapolis, 1895), 233; Duluth *Evening Herald*, 1 September 1894.

[2]Quoted in Elton T. Brown, *A History of the Great Minnesota Forest Fires* (St. Paul, 1894), 114-115.

[3]Quoted in *Ibid.*, 115, and Wilkinson, *Memorials*, 235.

[4]Wilkinson, *Memorials.*, 235.

[5]Gudmund Emanuel Akermark, *Eld-cyclonen eller Hinckley-branden*, William Johnson, trans. (1894; Askov, Minn., 1976), 2.

[6]Lucy N. A. Kelsey, *The September Holocaust: A Record of the Great Forest Fire of 1894* (Minneapolis, 1894), 70-76.

[7]The first two quotes are in *Ibid.*, 77; the third quote is in *The Hinckley Enterprise: Commemorated to the Survivors of the Great Hinckley Fire* (Hinckley, n.d.).

[8]Kelsey, *September Holocaust*, 78-79.

[9]Quoted in Wilkinson, *Memorials*, 269.

[10]*Ibid.*, 270.

[11]Kelsey, *September Holocaust*, 80-82.

[12]Quoted in Wilkinson, *Memorials*, 23.
[13]*Ibid.*, 52; Brown, *Great Minnesota Forest Fires*, 173.
[14]Quoted in Brown, *Ibid.*, 181.
[15]Quoted in Wilkinson, *Memorials*, 49.
[16]Quoted in Minneapolis *Tribune*, 4 September 1894.
[17]Brown, *Great Minnesota Forest Fires*, 165, 172, 201-202.
[18]Wilkinson, *Memorials*, 57-59.
[19]Quoted in *Ibid.*, 59.
[20]Quoted in Brown, *Great Minnesota Forest Fires*, 201-202.
[21]Quoted in Wilkinson, *Memorials*, 59.
[22]Brown, *Great Minnesota Forest Fires*, 212.
[23]Quoted in *Ibid.*, 203.
[24]Quoted in Wilkinson, *Memorials*, 132.
[25]The Sullivan quotes are in *Ibid.*, 150-151.
[26]Duluth *News Tribune*, 2 September 1894.
[27]Quoted in Wilkinson, *Memorials*, 171.
[28]*Ibid.*, 179.
[29]Quoted in *Ibid.*, 171-173.
[30]Brown, *Great Minnesota Forest Fires*, 118-119.
[31]Quoted in Wilkinson, *Memorials*, 158.
[32]*Ibid.*, 100-101.
[33]*Ibid.*, 23-24.
[34]Brown, *Great Minnesota Forest Fires*, 97-99; Minneapolis *Tribune*, 3 September 1894.
[35]Quoted in Brown, *Great Minnesota Forest Fires*, 203.
[36]Quoted in Wilkinson, *Memorials*, 191-192.
[37]Quoted in *Ibid.*, 213-215.
[38]Quoted in Brown, *Great Minnesota Forest Fires*, 203.
[39]Quoted in Wilkinson, *Memorials*, 211, 217.
[40]Quoted in *Ibid.*, 192.
[41]St. Paul *Pioneer Press*, 2 September 1894.

[1]Quoted in Rev. William Wilkinson, *Memorials of the Minnesota Forest Fires in the Year 1894 with a Chapter on the Forest Fires in Wisconsin in the Same Year* (Minneapolis, 1895), 192-193.
[2]*Ibid.*, 196-197.
[3]Elton T. Brown, *A History of the Great Minnesota Forest Fires* (St. Paul, 1894), 71; Duluth *Evening Herald*, 3 September 1894; Duluth *News Tribune*, 3 September 1894.
[4]Quoted in Wilkinson, *Memorials*, 236.
[5]*Ibid.*, 135-136.

[6]The Hurley quotes are in *Ibid.*, 197-199.

[7]Quoted in *Ibid.*, 216.

[8]Quoted in *Ibid.*, 225-226.

[9]Quoted in *Ibid.*, 217.

[10]The activities of the "Advanced Guard" are covered in detail in the Rush City *Post*, 7 September 1894.

[11]Quoted in Wilkinson, *Memorials*, 221-222.

[12]*Ibid.*, 222.

[13]Quoted in *Ibid.*, 101.

[14]Regan is quoted on pages 81-83 and Anderson on page 92 of *Ibid*. The old man is quoted in Gudmund Emanuel Akermark, *Eld-cyklonen eller Hinckley-branden*, William Johnson, trans. (1894; Askov, Minn., 1976), 72.

[15]Wilkinson, *Memorials*, 74-75.

[16]Brown, *Great Minnesota Forest Fires*, 100.

[17]Quoted in Wilkinson, *Memorials*, 135-136.

[18]Quoted in *Ibid.*, 146.

[19]Quoted in *Ibid.*, 240.

[20]Quoted in *Ibid.*, 237-238.

[21]*Ibid.*, 290.

[22]The quotes are from *Ibid.*, 216.

[23]Quoted in *Ibid.*, 132.

[24]Duluth *News Tribune*, 3 September 1894.

[25]Wilkinson, *Memorials*, 216-217.

[26]*Ibid.*, 299-300.

[27]*Ibid.*

[28]Wilkinson, *Memorials*, 239-240.

[29]Brown, *Great Minnesota Forest Fires*, 160-161.

[30]Stowe's quotes are in Wilkinson, *Memorials*, 218.

[31]Pine City *Pine County Pioneer*, 7 September 1894.

[32]Quoted in Wilkinson, *Memorials*, 222-223.

CHAPTER 7: "Aren't You Glad to See Somebody?"

[1]Elton T. Brown, *A History of the Great Minnesota Forest Fires* (St. Paul, 1894), 100-101.

[2]Quoted in Rev. William Wilkinson, *Memorials of the Minnesota Forest Fires in the Year 1894 with a Chapter on the Forest Fires in Wisconsin in the Same Year* (Minneapolis, 1895), 193.

[3]*Ibid.*, 306-307.

[4]Minneapolis *Tribune*, 2 September 1894.

[5]Wilkinson, *Memorials*, 191.
[6]Quoted in *Ibid.*, 193.
[7]Quoted in *Ibid.*, 270.
[8]Lucy N. A. Kelsey, *The September Holocaust: A Record of the Great Forest Fires of 1894* (Minneapolis, 1894), 84-89.
[9]Quoted in Wilkinson, *Memorials*, 92.
[10]Quoted in Duluth *News Tribune*, 29 August 1976.
[11]Wilkinson, *Memorials*, 92.
[12]Duluth *Evening Herald*, 3 September 1894.
[13]Wilkinson, *Memorials*, 305, 306.
[14]Brown, *Great Minnesota Forest Fires*, 105-106.
[15]Duluth *News Tribune*, 2 September 1894.
[16]Brown, *Great Minnesota Forest Fires*, 120-123.
[17]Kelsey, *September Holocaust*, 89-91.
[18]Mora *Kanabec County Times*, 7 September 1894.
[19]Quoted in Kelsey, *September Holocaust*, 91.
[20]Wilkinson, *Memorials*, 278.
[21]St. Cloud *Times*, 5 September 1894.
[22]Wilkinson, *Memorials*, 24.
[23]*Ibid.*, 338-339; Brown, *Great Minnesota Forest Fires*, 105-106.
[24]Wilkinson, *Memorials*, 154-155.
[25]Duluth *News Tribune*, 7 September 1894.
[26]Wilkinson, *Memorials*, 248-250, 301-302.
[27]Quoted in *Ibid.*, 212.
[28]*Ibid.*, 212-213.
[29]Quoted in Kelsey, *September Holocaust*, 92-93.
[30]*Ibid.*, 94.
[31]Quoted in Wilkinson, *Memorials*, 93.
[32]Quoted in *Ibid.*, 93-95.
[33]Quoted in *Ibid.*, 249.
[34]Duluth *News Tribune*, 4 September 1894.
[35]Wilkinson, *Memorials*, 250-251.

CHAPTER 8: "In Handling the Bodies We Made a Stretcher with Two Poles"

[1]Minneapolis *Tribune*, 3 September 1894.
[2]Quoted in Rev. William Wilkinson, *Memorials of the Minnesota Forest Fires in the Year 1894 with a Chapter on the Fires in Wisconsin in the Same Year* (Minneapolis, 1895), 339-340.

[3]*Ibid.*, 341.

[4]*Ibid.*, 321.

[5]*Ibid.*, 247-248; Elton T. Brown, *A History of the Great Minnesota Forest Fires* (St. Paul, 1894), 120-125.

[6]Quoted in Wilkinson, *Memorials*, 247.

[7]*Ibid.*, 189; Pine City *Pine County Pioneer*, 7 September 1894.

[8]Duluth *News Tribune*, 5 September 1894.

[9]Quoted in Wilkinson, *Memorials*, 273.

[10]*Ibid.*, 278-279; Mora *Kanabec County Times*, 7 September 1894.

[11]Wilkinson, *Memorials*, 207-209. The short quote about Norton's business practices is from this source.

[12]Brown, *Great Minnesota Forest Fires*, 73-85, has a summary of the course of the fires in Wisconsin.

[13]Wilkinson, *Memorials*, 249.

[14]Minneapolis *Tribune*, 4 September 1894; *Ibid.*, 366-367.

[15]Minneapolis *Tribune*, 4 September 1894.

[16]Brown, *Great Minnesota Forest Fires*, 179.

[17]Quoted in Wilkinson, *Memorials*, 95-96.

[18]Quoted in Minneapolis *Tribune*, 4 September 1894.

[19]*Ibid.*, 249, 305-307; Duluth *News Tribune*, 4 September 1894.

[20]Wilkinson, *Memorials*, 286; St. Cloud *Times*, 5 September 1894.

[21]Quoted in Wilkinson, *Memorials*, 29.

[22]*Ibid.*, 31.

[23]*Ibid.*, 309-311.

[24]Quoted in *Ibid.*, 311.

[25]*Ibid.*, 32-33. The Wilkinson quote is on page 33.

[26]Duluth *Evening Herald*, 3 September 1894.

[27]Quoted in Brown, *Great Minnesota Forest Fires*, 169.

[28]*Ibid.*, 94.

[29]Quoted in Minneapolis *Tribune*, 4 September 1894.

[30]Quoted in *Ibid.*

[31]Duluth *News Tribune*, 3 September 1894.

[32]*Ibid.*, 6 September 1894. The quotes are from this source.

[33]Quoted in *Ibid.*, 5 September 1894.

[34]*Ibid.*, Wilkinson, *Memorials*, 103-125, contains a "Death List."

[35]Brown, *Great Minnesota Forest Fires*, 216-217.

[36]*Ibid.*, 215.

[37]Duluth *Evening Herald*, 9 September 1894.

[38]Wilkinson, *Memorials*, 203.

[39]*Ibid.*, 203.

[40]Quoted in *Ibid.*, 203-205.

[41]Quoted in *Ibid.*, 205.

[42]Quoted in *Ibid.*, 205-207.

CHAPTER 9: "Heroism and Bravery"

[1]The report is printed in full in Rev. William Wilkinson, *Memorials of the Minnesota Forest Fires in the Year 1894 with a Chapter on the Forest Fires in Wisconsin in the Same Year* (Minneapolis, 1895), 1-67. It follows page 412 of the book and is numbered differently.

[2]*Ibid.*, 6-7, 23, 26.

[3]Quoted in *Ibid.*, 10.

[4]*Ibid.*

[5]*Ibid.*, 11-13.

[6]Quoted in Elton T. Brown, *A History of the Great Minnesota Forest Fires* (St. Paul, 1894), 123-124.

[7]Wilkinson, *Memorials*, 259-261.

[8]Duluth *Evening Herald*, 7 September 1894.

[9]Wilkinson, *Memorials*, 261. Wilkinson made the quoted statement about the refugees.

[10]*Ibid.*, 273-275.

[11]*Ibid.*, 281.

[12]*Ibid.*, 331-333.

[13]*Ibid.*, 352-354.

[14]*Ibid.*, 201.

[15]Quoted in *Ibid.*, 187.

[16]Quoted in *Ibid.*, 159-160.

[17]*Ibid.*, 161-163. The quotations are from this source.

[18]Duluth *Evening Herald*, 3 September 1894; Duluth *News Tribune*, 2 September 1894.

[19]Quoted in Wilkinson, *Memorials*, 133.

[20]Quoted in *Ibid.*, 146.

[21]Quoted in *Ibid.*, 151.

[22]Brown, *Great Minnesota Forest Fires*, before start of preface, n.p.

[23]Stewart H. Holbrook, *Burning of an Empire: The Story of American Forest Fires* (New York, 1943), 212-214.

[24]Wilkinson, *Memorials*, 398-401.

[25]Brown, *Great Minnesota Forest Fires*, 220. See also Frank R. Holmes, *Minnesota in Three Centuries*, 4 vols. (n.p., 1908), 223-229.

[26]Minneapolis *Tribune*, 4 September 1894.

[27]On 4 September 1894 the Duluth *News Tribune* estimated the death toll at at least 612.

[28]Brown, *Great Minnesota Forest Fires*, 138; *The Hinckley Enterprise: Commemorated to the Survivors of the Great Hinckley Fire* (Hinckley, n.d.).

[29]Lucy N. A. Kelsey, *The September Holocaust: A Record of the Great Forest Fire of 1894* (Minneapolis, 1894), 119.

[30]Wilkinson, *Memorials*, 71-72.

[31]Brown, *Great Minnesota Forest Fires*, 212-214; Gudmund Emanuel Akermark, *Eld-cyklonen eller Hinckley-branden*, William Johnson, trans. (1894; Askov, Minn., 1976), 90.

[32]Quoted in Wilkinson, *Memorials*, 195.

[33]William Watts Folwell, *A History of Minnesota*, 4 vols. (St. Paul, 1930), 213n.

[34]Akermark, *Hinckley-branden*, 10.

[35]Alice E. Andrews, ed., *Christopher C. Andrews: Pioneer in Forestry Conservation in the United States: for Sixty Years a Dominant Influence in the Public Affairs of Minnesota: Lawyer: Editor: Diplomat: General in the Civil War, Recollections: 1829-1922* (Cleveland, 1928), 285-291. The two Andrews quotations are from this source. So is the legislative provision.

[36]Quoted in Brown, *Great Minnesota Forest Fires*, 145.

[37]Brown, *Ibid.*, 205. See also Duluth *News Tribune*, 29 August 1976; *The Hinckley Enterprise*; Holbrook, *Burning of an Empire*, 19n; Kelsey, *September Holocaust*, 105-109; Wilkinson, *Memorials*, 51, 73, 79, 86.

For Further Reading

Many books that contain lists of disasters mention the Minnesota Forest Fire. These include encyclopedias and almanacs, plus such general references as James Cornell, *The Great International Disaster Book* (1976; New York, 1982); A. A. Hoehling, *Disaster: Major American Catastrophies* (New York, 1973); and Jay Robert Nash, *Darkest Hours: A Narrative Encyclopedia of World Wide Disasters from Ancient Times to the Present* (Chicago, 1976). References to the fire appear in other places. William E. Lass, *Minnesota: A Bicentennial History*, American Association for State and Local History (New York, 1977), mentions it in a discussion of the conservation movement in the Gopher State. There is a paragraph on the fire in Theodore C. Blegen, *Minnesota: A History of the State* (1963; Minneapolis, 1975). It receives brief notice in *Minnesota: A State Guide*, American Guide Series (New York, 1938). William Watts Folwell, *A History of Minnesota*, 4 vols. (St. Paul, 1930), indicates that the forest fire took place during the administration of Governor Knute Nelson. See also Frank L. Holmes, *Minnesota in Three Centuries*, 4 vols. (n.p., 1908). The Hinckley area is placed in the context of the lumber industry in Agnes M. Larson, *History of the White Pine Industry in Minnesota* (Minneapolis, 1949). Like most disasters — despite the public interest at the time of the tragedy — the Minnesota Forest Fire has received limited attention at best in recent times.

A few "enthusiastic amateurs" have written accounts of the fire. The most recent are Clark C. Peterson, *The Great Hinckley Fire* (1977; New York, 1980); Grace Swenson, *From the Ashes: The Story of the Hinckley Fire of 1894* (Stillwater, Minn., 1979). Peterson, a Hinckley resident and civic booster, published his book with the Exposition Press. It has a list of events associated with the fire, plus a promotional chapter on the annual Hinckley Korn and Klover Karnival. Swenson, a librarian and writer of youth books, states in her introduction that she has "inferred what is and what is not true." Another book, one published by Comet Press, Antone Anderson, *The Hinckley Fire* (New York, 1954), received little notice.

In general, professional historians have ignored forest fires. Indeed, scholarly works on the subject are few and far between. More representative are Betty G. Spencer, *The Big Blowup* (Caldwell, Id., 1956); Stan Cohen and Don Miller, *The Big*

Burn (Missoula, 1956); and Robert W. Wells, *Fire at Peshtigo* (Englewood Cliffs, N.J., 1968). Wells's study contains excellent material on the causes and different kinds of forest fires. Usually, only the largest and most destructive fires have received much in the way of attention. This has also been the case with coverage of other kinds of disasters.

Most "disaster books" have been produced by journalists and professional writers. Works on natural disasters include Marjory Stoneman, *Hurricane* (New York, 1958); John Duffy, *Epidemics in Colonial America* (Port Washington, N.J., 1972); David M. Ludlum, *Early American Tornadoes, 1558-1870*, American Meteorological Society (Boston, 1970); Joe McCarthy, *Hurricane* (New York, 1969); Charles Rosenberg, *The Cholera Years* (Chicago, 1962); and Gordon Thomas and Max Witts, *The San Francisco Earthquake* (New York, 1971). For man-made disasters — other than wars — see Paul Benzaquin, *Holocaust! The Cocoanut Grove Fire* (Boston, 1964); David McCullough, *The Johnstown Flood* (New York, 1968); and Thomas and Witts, *Shipwreck: The Strange Fate of the Morro Castle* (New York, 1972). A bibliography that includes these and other "disaster books," along with material on the impact of disasters on society, can be found in Cornell, *The Great International Disaster Book*. A problem in writing about any kind of disaster is frequently a lack of solid documentation. It is what might be called the "after-the-airplane-crash syndrome." No one knows about the last moments in the passenger cabin; all that remained in the aftermath was a ghastly heap of wreckage. Hence, the best contemporary account of the Peshtigo Fire was by a rescue worker: Rev. Peter Pernin, "The Great Peshtigo Fire," *Wisconsin Magazine of History*, 54:246-277 (Summer 1971). The Minnesota Forest Fire, because so many people escaped death, is a major exception.

A number of contemporary accounts appeared in the wake of the fire. Lucy N. A. Kelsey wrote about her experiences in *The September Holocaust: A Record of the Great Forest Fire of 1894* (Minneapolis, 1894). The Rev. William Wilkinson, a former chaplain of the Minnesota state legislature who was an early rescue worker in the fire district, compiled *Memorials of the Minnesota Forest Fires in the Year 1894 with a Chapter on the Forest Fires in Wisconsin in the Same Year* (Minneapolis, 1895). Wilkinson's lengthy book consists in the main of interviews he conducted and accounts he solicited from disaster participants. His work, which has a "Death List" of the victims, contains a wealth of primary material. Wilkinson paid little attention to organization, and there is no index. The dozens of individual accounts, several of which overlap, are scattered throughout the book, making it difficult to use. Another author who obtained eyewitness accounts was Elton T. Brown, *A History of the Great Minnesota Forest Fires: Sandstone, Mission Creek, Hinckley, Pokegama, and Skunk Lake* (St. Paul, 1894). His book has especially good material on the rescue effort. A Swedish-American newspaper editor produced a potboiler that emphasized the Swedish role in the forest fire: Gudmund Emanuel Akermark, *Eld-cyklonen eller Hinckley-branden*, William Johnson, trans. (1894; Askov, Minn., 1976). The books by Kelsey, Wilkinson, Brown, and Akermark all have 1894 or 1895 copyrights. In a sense, they wrote or compiled "instant history." Moreover, Wilkinson's and Brown's books represent early forays into what is now called "oral history." Some of the eyewitness evidence (the stilted language, for example, in several of the direct quotes) might tend to suggest after-the-fact doctoring. The same, however, can be said about most modern oral history transcripts. Usually the person interviewed receives an opportunity to edit the manuscript before it is put in final form for research use. What is important is not so much the preciseness of the language, but the correctness of the meaning and of the factual data. Then, too, whatever the pitfalls involved, firsthand accounts provide material and a flavor that cannot be conveyed in any other way.

Newspapers devoted whole issues to coverage of the fire. Of special note are the early September 1894 editions of the Duluth *News Tribune*, the Duluth *Evening Herald*, the Minneapolis *Tribune*, the St. Paul *Pioneer Press*, and the St. Paul *Daily Globe*. These journals sent their own correspondents into the fire zone, sometimes on the first relief trains. The national wire services naturally responded in kind. The first Associated Press and United Press dispatches did not appear in the two Duluth papers, because of disrupted telegraph service. The wire service stories are in Minneapolis and St. Paul journals. Of course, they appeared as well in newspapers throughout the rest of the nation and across the world, including the New York *Times* and the London *Times*. Local Minnesota papers, particularly those in communities on the fringe of the fire zone, provided good accounts of rescue efforts. The St. Cloud *Times* reported on St.

Cloud's extensive role in providing relief for fire victims. The Mora *Kanabec County Times*, the Pine City *Pine County Pioneer*, the Rush City *Post*, and the Appleton *Press* all kept their readers abreast of developments. Another paper, the Hinckley *Enterprise*, resumed publication a short time after the fire. Overall, the various newspapers constitute a valuable and essential source of information about the Minnesota Forest Fire.

Several other sources proved of use in studying the catastrophe. Alice E. Andrews, ed., *Christopher C. Andrews: Pioneer in Forestry Conservation in the United States: for Sixty Years a Dominant Influence in the Public Affairs of Minnesota: Lawyer: Editor: Diplomat: General in the Civil War, Recollections: 1829-1922* (Cleveland, 1928), has data on Andrews's long fight for pioneer foresty conservation reform in Minnesota. *The Hinckley Enterprise: Commemorated to the Survivors of the Great Hinckley Fire* (Hinckley, n.d.), published by the Hinckley Fire Museum, contains many eyewitness accounts. The museum, located in a former railroad station, has displays and a large mural relating to the fire. Edward W. Durant, "Lumbering and Steamboating on the St. Croix," in *Collections of the Minnesota Historical Society*, vol. 10, pt. 2 (St. Paul, 1905), has material on the extent of the pineries. Statistics on Pine County are available in a number of places, including *Compendium of the Eleventh Census: 1890*, pt. 2 (Washington, 1894); *Report on the Statistics of Churches in the United States at the Eleventh Census: 1890, vol. 9* (Washington, 1895); *Report on the Statistics of Agriculture in the United States at the Eleventh Census: 1890*, vol. 5 (Washington, 1896); *Report on Manufacturing Industries in the United States at the Eleventh Census: 1890*, vol. 6, pt. 1 (Washington, 1895). A colorful account of the Minnesota Forest Fire can be found in Stewart H. Holbrook, *Burning an Empire: The Story of American Forest Fires* (New York, 1943). For a unique view on the cultural aspects of fire in history see Stephen J. Pyne, *Fire in America: A Cultural History of Wildland and Rural Fire* (Princeton, 1982). A variety of rich and varied materials proved invaluable in studying the Minnesota Forest Fire.

INDEX

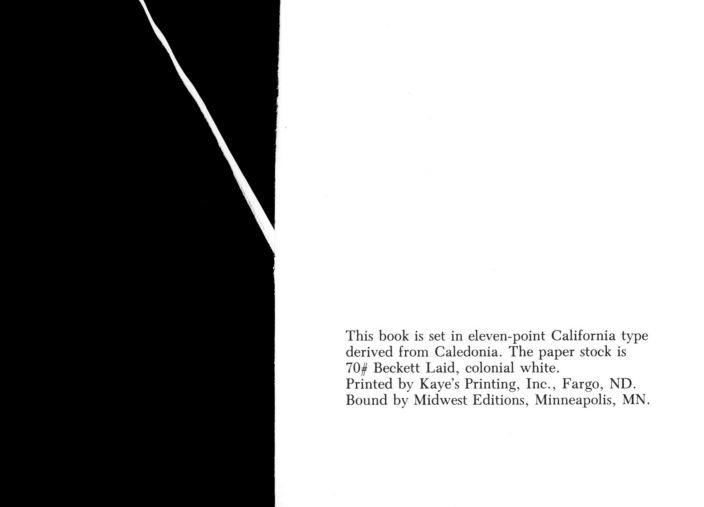

This book is set in eleven-point California type
derived from Caledonia. The paper stock is
70# Beckett Laid, colonial white.
Printed by Kaye's Printing, Inc., Fargo, ND.
Bound by Midwest Editions, Minneapolis, MN.

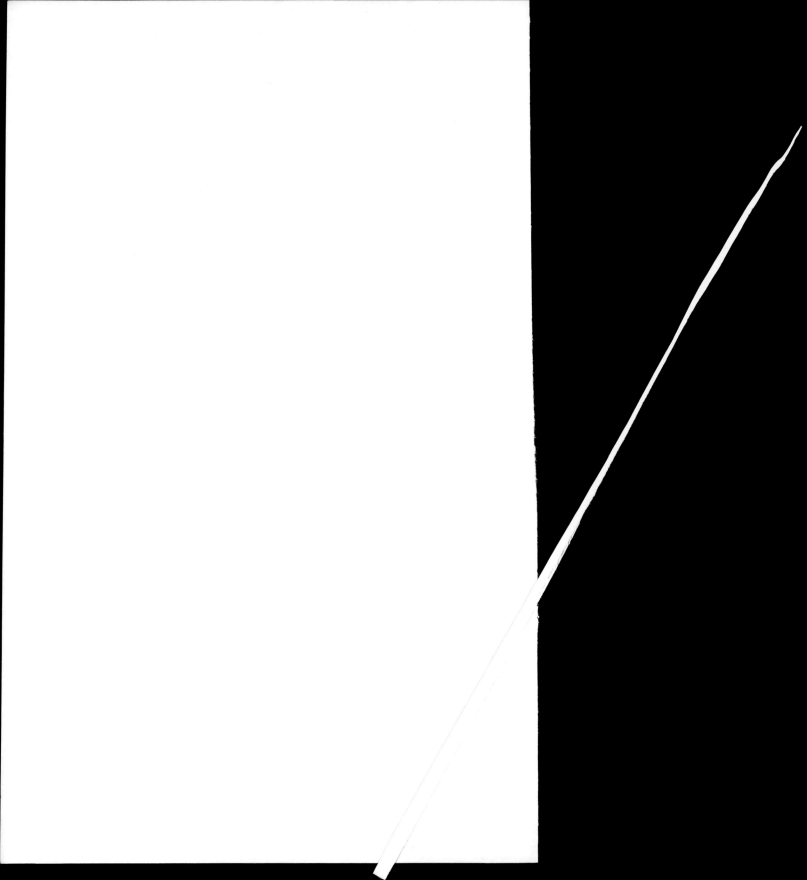